Food Combining
for Health Cookbook

Doris Grant knew Dr William Howard Hay and introduced the Hay system of eating to Britain. Now in her ninety-sixth year, she is still full of energy and vitality and writes widely on health issues.

Jean Joice worked as a radio and television producer specializing in health topics and has written extensively about herbs. A lifelong wholefooder, she met Doris when making a TV film about her some thirty years ago and they have worked closely together ever since.

Jackie Le Tissier holds the esteemed Cordon Vert Cookery Diploma and first began food combining for health reasons. A creative and accomplished cook, she is also a vegetarian.

While grateful for all the comments and suggestions that they have received over the years from readers, the authors regret that they are no longer able to reply personally to letters.

Food Combining
for Health Cookbook

Jean Joice and Jackie Le Tissier

Thorsons

Thorsons
An Imprint of HarperCollins*Publishers*
77–85 Fulham Palace Road
Hammersmith, London W6 8JB

The Thorsons website is
www.thorsons.com

Published by Thorsons 1994
This revised edition 2000

10 9 8 7 6 5 4 3 2

A catalogue record for this book is available
from the British Library

ISBN 0 7225 4033 7

Printed and bound in Great Britain by
Martins the Printers Limited, Berwick upon Tweed

Contents

Acknowledgements

We should like to thank our families and the friends who gallantly ate their way through the recipes for their very helpful comments and suggestions, not forgetting the essential contribution of Honey and Tess, the Clumber Spaniels who dutifully demolished the less successful experiments.

Special mentions to vegetarian 'guinea-pigs' Betty and John Middlebrook. Thanks must also go to Craig Alexander and Jay Hagger for their continued support and provision of office facilities, and to Guernsey Fresh Herbs for the abundant supply of homegrown herbs.

We are grateful to Sonia Bell and Helen Breach for typing many of the recipes and notes; to Liz Godfray for her careful and constructive assessment of the manuscript; to Sarah Sutton, Senior Editor at Thorsons and her colleagues Michele Turney and Kate Davey for their unflagging enthusiasm and hard work on the project, and to Wanda Whiteley for her encouragement.

Lastly we thank Rose Elliot for her continuing encouragement and permission to reproduce two of her original recipes, and, as always, our grateful thanks to 'the founder of the feast', Doris Grant, who introduced both of us to the Hay System and whose inspiring example and warm friendship over many years has enabled both of us to achieve more than we would ever have thought possible.

Foreword

As I am constantly pointing out, food combining is in no sense a wearisome diet, it is a delicious way of eating for health.

Nothing could better confirm this fact than the wealth of delicious recipes by Jean and Jackie in their beautifully presented new cookbook. The recipes are so unusual and innovative that they will inspire cooks everywhere, be they food combiners, wholefooders or otherwise, to rush into the kitchen and start creating culinary masterpieces. The secret of this inspiration is an unlisted but very effective ingredient in all the recipes – enthusiasm.

Apart from the excellent recipes, the book is also a blueprint for a healthy and enjoyable lifestyle based on Dr Hay's 'essentially holistic teaching'. As the authors point out, this teaching stresses an all-important fact: that it is not only what you eat but what you think that is necessary for the whole person.

Jean's beautifully and simply written chapters contain easily understood information about the Hay System, what it is, and eminently practical instructions on how to put it into practice. There are notes, too, on a number of minor stumbling blocks which can beset the path of newcomers to the Hay scene, such as the meaning of 'acid-forming' and 'alkali-forming', and how to use foods so termed to maintain the correct chemical balance of the body.

She has also explained the importance of fruit in food combining. This cannot be sufficiently stressed. Dr Hay regarded fruit as the number one priority among the foods necessary for health, and his advice was to eat it at every meal and always to eat it raw (if ripe).

The outstanding feature of this book, however, is the simplicity with which the recipes are arranged in sections – protein, starch and alkaline – so that complete meals can be easily put together without the need to consult time-consuming and daunting columns of foods or charts. This simplicity would have delighted Dr Hay.

Thanks to the outstanding success of earlier food combining books and the ever-increasing number of their readers who have been clamouring for more recipes, I predict that there will be an enormous welcome for Jean and Jackie's beautiful new cookbook, and I wish it all success.

Doris Grant

Introduction

Although it is now more than a decade since Doris Grant and I joined forces to write *Food Combining for Health*, the number of Hay enthusiasts is steadily increasing as one successful adherent after another recommends food combining to friends.

Soon after its publication in 1984 the book became a best seller and, since the mass market edition was launched in 1991, it has featured consistently in the top 10 best-selling paperback manuals. This in itself is a more or less unheard of success for a book that has been on the market for so long.

Perhaps the reason lies in the fact that it is not just another diet book, but a very practical guide to a healthier lifestyle based on Dr Hay's essentially holistic teaching. For he taught that it is not only what you eat, but what you *think*, that adds up to the health of the whole person, that regeneration and returning vitality can only come through correct eating, exercise and rest, thus enabling body and mind to function harmoniously and accommodate the stresses and strains of twentieth-century life.

Over the years Doris and I have received many enthusiastic letters telling us about recoveries, often dramatic, from allergies, migraine, arthritis, colitis, indigestion and many other medically diagnosed conditions, and all testifying to increased vitality and energy.

One that really said it all arrived only a few months ago:

> Since Christmas my children and I have followed the advice given (in Food Combining for Health) not because we had any particular problems but for the long-term general good of our health. This has had the unlooked-for advantage for me of the easy and gradual loss of one stone (14 pounds) in weight, and also the saving of quite a lot of money from food bills which now goes towards more luxury fruit and vegetables such as strawberries and asparagus.

This rather proves Dr Hay's point that given a chance in the form of eating as nature intended, the body will heal itself and this includes weight loss as part of a normalizing process. It also shows that food combining need not be expensive as so much money can be saved by cutting out processed and junk foods.

So whatever your motive in reading this, whether to resolve a specific health problem, to lose weight, or just to feel better, be assured that from the hundreds of letters and other evidence received, food combining really does work.

Another happy outcome has been Jackie Le Tissier's recovery from a painful arthritic condition known as ankylosing spondylitis after she had adopted the system. In due course she adapted it for vegetarians and wrote *Food Combining for Vegetarians*, another success story.

This cookbook is the result of a happy collaboration with Jackie in response to an ever-growing demand for more Hay recipes and ideas. It is also written for those who prefer a practical approach and who do not want to be bothered with too many lists and charts. The whole idea is to keep it simple as Dr Hay originally intended and, in three words, just do it.

Jean Joice

The Hay System
What it is and how to put it into practice

The main purpose of this book is to simplify the planning and preparation of compatible meals in accordance with the principles of food combining taught by Dr William Howard Hay. A detailed description of his system and the rationale behind it has already been given in earlier books: *Food Combining for Health* by Doris Grant and Jean Joice (Thorsons, 1984) and *Food Combining for Vegetarians* by Jackie Le Tissier (Thorsons, 1992).

This book aims to give only a brief introduction to the Hay design for healthy eating so that simple and delicious compatible meals can be prepared right from the word go without having to refer to detailed explanations or lengthy lists or charts. There are plenty of recipe ideas for wholefooders and vegetarians alike, but it is suggested that reference to the two books mentioned above should be made for a more in-depth study of the Hay System and how it can work for you, and also to extend your recipe repertoire.

Food Classification

Dr Hay classified foods into three types according to their chemical requirements for efficient digestion and assimilation. These three types are:

1 Alkali-forming foods such as fruits and vegetables. By alkali-forming we mean the end-product of such foods after digestion. Even 'acid' tasting fruits such as lemons yield alkaline salts in the body.
2 Concentrated proteins (20 per cent or more) such as meat, game, fish, eggs or cheese. These foods are acid-forming in their final end-product in the body.
3 Concentrated carbohydrates or starch foods (which are also acid-forming) – grains, bread and all foods containing flour, and all sugars

and foods containing sugar (sucrose), but not the naturally occurring sugars found in fruit.

The recipes in this book are grouped under these three classifications – Alkaline, Protein or Starch – so that whole meals can be prepared from each section to give a well-combined meal of each type.

Dr Hay's theory was that although both protein and starch foods are acid-forming in their final end-product in the body, they need *different* conditions for *digestion* and should never be combined at the same meal.

Acid/Alkaline Balance

This distinction between acid-forming and alkali-forming foods is of fundamental importance to the Hay system of food combining, the reason being that the body contains alkaline and acid mineral salts in the proportion of four to one. To maintain this natural balance we should eat the foods that yield corresponding amounts of alkaline and acid salts. The alkaline foods are the bulky foods containing a great deal of water – all green and root vegetables, saladings and herbs, and all fruits. Although citrus fruits are often referred to as acid fruits, acid-tasting must not be confused with acid-*forming*, which they are not; the acid fruits (except

---

The Hay Rules for Health

1 Starches and sugars should not be eaten with proteins and acid fruits at the same meal.
2 Vegetables, salads and fruits (whether acid or sweet, if correctly combined) should form the major part of the diet.
3 Proteins, starches and fats should be eaten in small quantities.
4 Only whole grains and unprocessed starches should be used and all refined and processed foods should be eliminated from the diet. This particularly applies to white flour and sugar and all foods containing them, all highly processed fats such as margarine and all highly coloured and sweetened foods and drinks such as orange squash and cola.
5 An interval of not less than four hours should elapse between meals of different character.

Food Combining for Health Cookbook

plums) are the best source of alkaline salts. Non-acid fruits are referred to as sweet fruits, and a full list of both acid and sweet fruits can be found in the Table of Compatible Foods (page 20).

The acid-forming foods, as already described, are the concentrated proteins (meat, poultry, game, fish, eggs, shellfish and cheese) and the concentrated starches (bread and all foods made with flour, grains of all kinds [except millet] and sugar in all forms).

Too great a proportion of these foods upsets the natural mineral balance of the body and contributes to ill-health – especially rheumatism and arthritis.

Rule 1

The first rule, which can be summed up in Doris Grant's slogan *Don't mix foods that fight*, is the most important one to remember. Following this rule allows foods to digest in the most efficient way and can bring about dramatic health benefits in an amazingly short time.

To explain briefly: starches, i.e. the foods containing concentrated starches (20 per cent or more) such as grains, bread, cereals, potatoes and sugars need an alkaline medium for digestion. This starts in the mouth where an enzyme called ptyalin splits the starches ready for their further digestion in the small intestine. All starch foods should be well chewed and mixed with saliva before swallowing.

Protein foods, on the other hand, need an acid medium for digestion. These foods (meat, fish, cheese, eggs and poultry) stimulate the production of hydrochloric acid when they enter the stomach and if they are mixed with starchy foods (with their alkalis) the acid medium is partly neutralized and the proteins incompletely digested.

Sir John Mills recounts in his foreword to *Food Combining for Health* how the application of this rule cured the 'man-sized' duodenal ulcer that had invalided him out of the army. Within six weeks he was able to start work on a film.

Rules 2 and 3

Rules two and three concern the *balance* of the diet. Doris Grant once wrote 'cultivate the salad habit as if your life depended on it – it does!' It is the protective power of raw salads and vegetables with their rich store of vitamins, minerals and alkali-forming properties which helps to give the correct balance for top level health. By the same token we need only small quantities of the acid-forming proteins and starches, and the neutral fats. The ratio to aim for is 4 to 1, alkaline to acid.

Rule 4

Rule four is most important. Every effort should be made to cut out sugar, white flour and all foods containing them, and all processed and artificially coloured foods. It is these highly refined foods, robbed of their naturally occurring fibre, that lead to the over-consumption that is now thought to be responsible for so many of our Western degenerative diseases: coronary heart disease, diabetes, obesity, cancer of the colon and dental caries.

The concept of a single *saccharine disease*, i.e. related to the consumption of sugar and white flour, was brilliantly described by Surgeon Captain T. L. Cleave in his book of the same title. The risks to children under 18 from widely advertised and heavily sugared products and drinks have been examined by Elbie Lebrecht in her books *Sugar-free Desserts, Drinks and Ices* and *Sugar-free Cooking.* We urge every parent to read her devastatingly clear account of the dangers to our children of a high consumption of sugar.

Excess sugar can also affect mood and behaviour, particularly in children and adolescents. It can be a contributory cause of hyperactivity and, with white flour, can cause hypoglycaemia and the production of too much insulin, leading to faintness, hunger, irritability and sudden changes of mood.

We now consume on average about 1 kg/2lb of sugar per week. Two hundred years ago it used to take us a whole year to get through the amount of sugar we now eat in two weeks. We are simply not adapted to this flood of sugar and it is causing an appalling amount of damage to our health. (However, giving up sugar entirely is not easy, and we have included a little honey in a few of our recipes.)

Putting the Rules into Practice

The easiest way to put these rules into practice and achieve the ideal ratio of four to one between the essential alkali-forming foods and the acid-forming foods is to arrange the day's meals so that animal protein is eaten only once a day, cereal starches once a day, and the third meal consists of raw fruit only or raw fruit with milk or yoghurt. Most people eat too much protein and starch, particularly the latter which is found in so many convenience foods.

All meals should rely heavily on vegetables and fruits; even the protein or starch meals should contain only modest amounts of these latter ingredients, the main emphasis of the meal being on raw salads, vegetable soups or lightly steamed or stir-fried green or root vegetables. In fact, contrary to the usual arrangement of meat flanked by small portions of cooked vegetables, the meal should be a feast of vegetables garnished with the meat, fish or cheese, or the rice or pasta. Ideally it is better to eat meat no more than three times a week and to eat concentrated protein once every other day, alternating with a concentrated starch meal. For top level health one day a week on alkali-forming foods only helps to give maximum protection from the many pollutants in our environment.

The Recipes

All the recipes in this book are classified according to these principles and grouped together for ease of reference. Thus in Section One – the Alkaline Meal – the recipes are composed only of alkaline-forming ingredients and each recipe is compatible with every other recipe in that section so that a complete alkaline meal can be assembled without having to consult lists or charts. The same arrangement holds good for the protein and starch sections.

A well-combined meal plan should look something like this:

Breakfast

The best time for the important alkaline meal of the day.
Fresh fruit in season, or fruit with a pot of plain yoghurt and a tablespoon of fresh or stabilized wheatgerm.

A hot drink such as weak tea, herb tea, dandelion coffee or real (not instant) coffee, if you must. Make coffee by the filter method and serve with hot milk (half and half).

Light Meal

Usually at midday chosen from the starch section.
A salad of your choice, potatoes cooked in their skins served with butter and a steamed vegetable; a sweet fruit such as banana to follow.

For a packed lunch a salad sandwich made with wholemeal (wholewheat) bread and butter, a thermos of vegetable soup and a sweet fruit to follow would make a satisfying meal.

Main Meal

Chosen from the protein section.
This meal can include a salad of fresh raw vegetables and/or a vegetable soup, a moderate portion of fish, meat, chicken, game, eggs or cheese, and lightly steamed green or root vegetables, but not potatoes. This can be followed by any of the fresh acid fruits such as apples, pears or oranges, served without sugar.

Only one protein dish should be served per meal – that is, you would not serve a meat dish followed by cheese or another concentrated protein. If you prefer to eat your main meal at midday, the light meal can be taken in the evening and can either be starch or protein.

As far as preparation time for these meals is concerned the maxim must be *fresh, fast and flavoursome.* Meals containing such a high proportion of raw fruits and vegetable should use the freshest ingredients possible, and in our recipes we have tried to keep preparation and cooking times to a minimum. Simple meals consisting of one main dish with a salad or lightly steamed vegetables, followed by a compatible fruit, are far less taxing on the digestive system; the conventional three-course dinner of first course, main course and pudding should be regarded as an occasional treat or for entertaining.

Notes on Foods and Equipment for the Hay Kitchen

The Importance of Fruit in Food Combining

Dr Hay listed foods in the following order of importance:

- Fruits
- Raw salad foods and leafy greens
- Root vegetables
- Grains
- Proteins

He maintained that all the elements for top-level health can be supplied by fruits, greens, roots and milk, and that large quantities of protein and cereal foods can overburden the metabolism.

He recommended that as far as possible fruit should be eaten raw, provided it is fully ripe. In this way it is both cleansing and alkaline-forming, yielding its full complement of vitamins and minerals. Cooked fruit is not recommended; heat destroys vitamin C and the sugar with which it is so often prepared makes it very acid-forming.

Some versions of food combining recommend that fruit should be eaten alone and not following a starch or protein meal. Their argument is that the digestion of fruit, which is fast when eaten on its own, is retarded by the slower digesting proteins or starches, resulting in fermentation.

Dr Hay always said that provided the fruit was properly combined with the meal, i.e. acid fruit with proteins and sweet fruit with starches, there would be no such fermentation. Furthermore such a prohibition greatly lessens the enjoyment of a meal for most people and does nothing to encourage a lifelong adherence to this way of eating.

Dr Max Bircher-Benner, of Muesli fame, also advocated eating raw food, including fruit, at the beginning of a meal to improve digestion.

Ideally fruit should be eaten at every meal; to limit fruit to between meals may well reduce the amount eaten overall, especially the amount of citrus fruit eaten and this, in correct combination, does more than any other type of fruit to increase the vital alkaline reserve of the body. (The only fruit that should be eaten alone is melon, which does not digest well with any other food, however on its own it makes a delicious breakfast.) In-between-meal fruit snacks are not always practical for many people and can *cause* digestive problems if eaten too near to a meal with which they are not compatible. Moreover, they break the fifth Hay rule (that an interval of not less than four hours should be allowed between meals of different character).

In conversation with Doris Grant many years ago, Dr Hay insisted that he had invented no new diet but had adapted one founded on ancient physiological laws long forgotten. All he did was to present these dietary laws in a form that would be practical for a twentieth-century lifestyle. He also felt that unless the diet was as practical as possible, eliminating unnecessary or unimportant rules, people would not stick to it or might become over-preoccupied with their food and health.

Doris herself has now been following Dr Hay's precepts for over 65 years. During this time she has received countless letters from food-combining enthusiasts confirming the great improvement in health and energy that this system brings about.

Recent UK Government guidelines confirm the protective role of fresh fruit and vegetables in the diet. In countries where their consumption is high, e.g. Italy and Greece, the incidence of coronary heart disease and some cancers is markedly lower than those in the UK. Moreover, a recent study of 11,348 adults in the US reported in the journal *Epidemiology* by Dr James Estrom found that men with an intake of 300–400 mg per day of vitamin C had 45 per cent lower heart disease rates than men with an intake of less than 50 mg. There was also some evidence that vitamin C reduced cancer rates. To consume the high levels of the vitamin shown in the low-risk group would mean eating fresh fruit and vegetables five times a day.

Milk and Milk Products

Milk, a complete protein, should be regarded as a food, not a drink, and used sparingly by adults. In humans (adults especially) it can cause allergies, digestive disorders and persistent catarrh.

Raw, untreated milk is an alkaline food but becomes acid-forming when subjected to heat as in pasteurization or sterilization. It is best combined with fruit or salads and should only be used in small quantities with starches and cereals. It should never be taken with a meal containing meat.

Yoghurt, being easier to digest, is a better alternative for adults, particularly the elderly.

In all recipes where the use of cheese is indicated a vegetarian cheese can be substituted.

Cream, diluted, is an excellent alternative to milk, and because it is a fat it is neutral (see Table of Compatible Foods, page 20) and can be used as a milk substitute in starch recipes. Simply water down cream to the desired flavour (it really does taste like milk) and use as you would milk for your day-to-day requirements – over cereals, in starch sauces, rice or macaroni puddings, etc. There is no need to worry about increased fat or cholesterol in the diet – the cream is so watered down by volume that you are taking no more fat content than if you were drinking milk. Even where undiluted cream is used, and it is almost a necessity in the Hay diet, it is less concentrated than other fats and little is needed.

Eggs

Whole fresh eggs are a wonderful protein food, but the whites are very acid-forming. Used occasionally, in the same way as meat or fish for protein meals, they are perfectly acceptable. Egg yolks, however, are high in fat and thus a 'neutral' food, and can therefore be combined with all meals.

What about Calcium?

There is a good deal of concern these days about the ever-increasing incidence of osteoporosis – the bone-thinning condition that is appearing in younger and younger Caucasian women, not only those past the menopause. Although milk is a good source of calcium, the mineral essential for building strong bones and teeth, it is not always well absorbed (though this problem should improve when foods are properly combined). Many other foods are also good sources, however:

- Cheese and yoghurt
- All greens, especially broccoli
- Nuts and seeds, particularly almonds and sesame seeds
- Sea vegetables

- Fresh fish, also canned salmon and sardines
- Wholegrains

Vegetables and Salads

These should form the most important part of the Hay diet. All saladings and green and root vegetables are alkali-forming and, with the exception of potatoes and Jerusalem artichokes, can be combined with all recipes. Whenever possible buy organically grown vegetables, saladings and fruit. All fruits and vegetables should be thoroughly washed; in the case of apples and pears, unless organically grown, it is best to peel them. This also applies to mushrooms, unless you are very sure of their origin.

In order to avoid unnecessary repetition in the recipe sections that follow, here is a list of many of these salad ingredients and/or vegetables:

Asparagus
Aubergines (Eggplant)
Avocados
Beetroot (Beet)
Broccoli
Brussels sprouts
Cabbage (all types)
Calabrese
Carrots
Cauliflower
Celeriac
Celery
Chard
Chicory (Endive)
Chives
Courgettes (Zucchini)
Cucumber
Dandelion leaves
Fresh green peas
Kale
Kohlrabi

Leeks
Lettuce
Marrow (Squash)
Mushrooms
Mustard and Cress
Onions
Parsnips
Peppers (green, red and yellow)
Radishes
Runner (or string) Beans
Salsify
Seakale
Shallots
Spinach
Spring greens
Spring onions (Scallions)
Swedes (Rutabaga)
Tomatoes
Turnips
Watercress

Lightly steamed or shredded stir-fried vegetables are compatible with all three food classifications and a further selection of salads and vegetables is included within each section. It is useful to have a basic green salad recipe which will combine happily with any other type of food and which can be added to provided that the extra ingredients are compatible with the meal you are serving. A basic green salad recipe is set out for your guidance below.

Basic Green Salad
The important thing with a green salad is to have a variety of saladings, both in appearance and texture, so that it looks interesting and refreshing and offers a range of different flavours. It goes without saying that all the ingredients must be really fresh. If you are basing your salad on lettuce, use a crisp, firm variety such as Webb's Wonderful, Iceberg, Little Gem or the large type of Cos Lettuce.

1 clove garlic

a bowl of crisp lettuce, or young spinach
  or chard leaves

1 bunch watercress

½ cucumber, peeled and sliced

2 spring onions (scallions) or ½ shallot,
  finely chopped

chopped fresh herbs as available

dressing – compatible with the type of
  meal being served

1 Rub your salad bowl with the cut garlic clove.
2 Arrange the prepared ingredients in the bowl, tearing large leaves into smaller pieces.
3 Toss with the dressing just before serving.

This basic green salad can be varied with the addition of sprouted seeds such as alfalfa, lamb's lettuce (mâche) in the spring, chopped celery, chicory (endive), blanched dandelion leaves, rocket or a few young lovage leaves.

If you have a garden we recommend Joy Larkom's books *The Salad Garden* and *Oriental Vegetables* (see Bibliography). If you live near a good supermarket many now sell delicious fresh pre-packed salads which offer colourful, unusual salad leaves and save the trouble of buying larger quantities of, say, six different salad plants.

Seeds of herbs and salad vegetables can be obtained from Suffolk Herbs; their extensive list includes such delights as the spicy salad Rocket, a non-bolting cut-and-come-again lettuce called Green Salad Bowl, and a truly wonderful red arrow head oak-leaf lettuce called Cocarde which seems to go on producing tasty leaves all through summer.

Fats and Oils/Butter and Margarine

The highly promoted margarines high in polyunsaturated fats can be very damaging to health. We certainly *do* need these polyunsaturated fatty acids in our diet but they occur naturally in fresh food such as seeds and nuts, vegetables and fish. When vegetable oils are used to produce margarine the unsaturated fats are changed chemically to saturated fats by the process of hydrogenation and are far less healthy than the naturally occurring saturated fats in fresh farm butter. A recently published 10-year study by Harvard Medical School concludes that the hydrogenated vegetable oils in margarines actually *contribute* to the occurrence of coronary heart disease. So, wherever possible it is best to avoid all highly processed margarines and spreads.

It is, however, understood that in the vegan, and often the vegetarian diet, margarine will be the choice of fat in order to avoid the consumption of animal products. In those recipes where butter only is indicated a suitable margarine can be substituted instead. There are now a few margarines available on the market containing a high percentage of non-hydrogenated mono-unsaturated fats. Read all labels carefully and use these margarines in preference to those containing saturated fats.

All fats and oils are neutral and can be combined with all foods. Throughout this book we have used cold pressed olive oil or unrefined sunflower oil and unsalted butter for our recipes. Butter and olive oil, which are monounsaturated fats, are more stable at higher temperatures than other vegetable oils and less liable to rancidity.

The Hay diet is low in fat and eliminates most hidden fats (those found in biscuits, cakes and sweet products) but is rich in those fats that provide vitamin A, and the essential fatty acids that form part of every cell in the body.

Olive Oil

Olive oil, which features so strongly in the Mediterranean diet, appears to have a protective effect on the heart and arteries. Certainly the incidence of coronary heart disease and some cancers is lower in countries where olive oil is widely used.

We use several varieties of olive oil: an ordinary cold-pressed olive oil for stir-frying, a mild flavoured extra virgin oil for everyday use, and a high quality cold-pressed extra virgin oil for salads and other special dishes. There is a wide variety in taste between the oils from different countries and it is fun to shop around to find the ones that you prefer. Always keep the olive oil in a well corked bottle in a dark, cool place to prevent rancidity.

For cooking, unsalted butter is less likely to brown; adding a little olive oil to the butter will also help to prevent this.

Stock (Bouillon)

We very rarely use stock (bouillon), even a vegetable stock (bouillon), in preparing soups, preferring to let the individual flavours of the vegetables speak for themselves. It is interesting that latterly the late Jane Grigson was an advocate of this view. If, however, you do wish to use stock (bouillon), you can make your own or use one of the excellent vegetable stocks (bouillons) available in cube, powder or liquid form from your local health food store or supermarket.

Fruits and Dried Fruits

Where the rind of a lemon or orange is needed, try to use organic fruit or at least fruit that is unwaxed. Similarly, unless you know that the dessert fruit you are eating is organic, it is best to peel it. Whenever possible use unsulphured dried fruits, preferably sun-dried. If you are not sure about the origin of your dried fruit then blanch it by covering it with boiling water for a few minutes; pour this water away, cover the fruit with fresh boiling water and leave until it is ready for use.

Herbs

The use of fresh herbs in salads and cooked dishes can transform them into something really special. If possible grow your own; most culinary herbs need very little space and if you have no garden many can be grown in pots on the window sill. Some herbs dry well but most are best gathered fresh and, happily, more and more fresh herbs are becoming available in the supermarkets. These are some of our favourite herbs used in the recipes in this book.

Basil

Essential for tomato salad and many Italian dishes. It is an annual and does not dry well but it is possible to grow a good crop in pots. To preserve the basil flavour for use in winter, steep a handful of leaves in a bottle of extra virgin olive oil.

Bay Leaves

Can be used fresh or dry. If you or a friend have a tree, you can dry or freeze the leaves for winter use. Use in casseroles or with parsley and thyme to make a bouquet garni.

Chervil

Another annual that can be added to salads. It goes well in soups and is especially good in egg dishes.

Chives

These make a good ornamental border in the herb garden. Pick them when young – a little goes a long way. The pretty mauve flowers are edible and can be sprinkled over salads in summer.

Coriander

Fresh coriander leaves are now more readily available in supermarkets and ethnic shops. They have a pungent aroma that lifts a mixed green salad. If you grow your own, choose the variety cilantro. This has more leaves than other varieties, which tend to go rapidly to seed. The seeds are useful but different in flavour from the leaves.

Dill

A must for many fish dishes. The fronds add their special flavour to poached fish and potato salads or sauces based on soured cream. Again, the seeds are useful but different.

Lovage

You need a garden for this as it is a large perennial plant and one is enough! The young leaves are a good addition to a green salad in early spring and it is excellent in soups.

Marjoram and its wild cousin Oregano

These are easy to grow perennials and add tremendously to tomato dishes. Dried oregano is reasonably successful.

Mint

There are many different varieties to choose from but Bowles' mint is one of the best flavoured for the kitchen. Plant in a large pot or a corner where its growth can be controlled. Good with lamb, in chilled cucumber soup, in salads and many other dishes.

Parsley

We like to grow the flat-leaved continental variety as well as the moss-curled. There really is no substitute for fresh parsley and it is well worth protecting it during the winter so that you are never without it.

Rosemary

One of Jean's favourite herbs but very powerful. If she starts to weed her rosemary border with a headache, she finds her headache is gone by the time the job is finished – rosemary is marvellously aromatic and can be relied upon to clear the head! A small sprig or two is wonderful with spring lamb.

Salad Burnet

A very useful little plant which remains green all through winter. The leaves are very decorative for use in salads and sauces and have a slight cucumber flavour.

Salad Rocket

A superb salad plant whose leaves have a delicious spicy flavour. Use it to add interest to a mixed green salad. It does very well in a pot.

Sorrel

Much prized in France but neglected in Britain. It is very easy to grow, a hardy perennial and the young leaves in spring are good in salads or with eggs, as in an omelette. A little goes a long way as it has diuretic properties!

Tarragon
If growing your own, make sure you have the French variety. Russian tarragon lacks the wonderful subtle flavour of French tarragon. It seems to have a special affinity with chicken and eggs and is very useful in cream sauces.

Thyme
There are so many kinds to choose from but lemon thyme or the more usual *Thymus vulgaris* – ordinary culinary thyme – are the most useful in the kitchen.

Winter Savory
A small and perennial cousin of summer savory which goes so well with all bean dishes, especially broad (fava) beans, and is known as the bean herb. You can grow winter savory in a pot or in the garden and it does much the same job as its cousin but you need less of it.

Spices

Dr Hay warned against highly spiced foods that could irritate the digestive tract, but a judicious use of spices adds subtle flavour and helps to reduce the use of salt. Spices must be fresh, so only buy a little of any one at a time. For preference buy the whole seeds and grind just before using.

Cinnamon
Cinnamon sticks can be used in the cooking process and removed. However they are difficult to grind at home and if you need ground (powdered) cinnamon it is best to buy a small quantity and use it up quickly.

Cloves
Buy whole cloves and grind your own in a spice mill, or crush using a pestle and mortar.

Coriander
Coriander is useful in savoury dishes, and a few seeds freshly ground add a new dimension to ratatouille.

Ginger
Use fresh ginger root for preference. Peel and chop finely before adding to stir-fry dishes.

Mace
Mace subtly enhances the flavour of many winter vegetables such as cauliflower. It is best to use blade mace; if you buy ground get only a small quantity as it soon loses its flavour.

Nutmeg
Buy nutmeg whole and grate a little as needed. It transforms spinach and mushroom dishes.

Paprika
Made from dried sweet red peppers, paprika stales very quickly so buy only a little at a time. It goes well in dishes cooked with yoghurt or soured cream.

Pepper
Indispensable in the kitchen; we usually use black peppercorns freshly ground, but white peppercorns can also be used. The black peppercorns are the dried unripe fruit; the white peppercorns have been harvested when almost ripe.

Vanilla Pods
These can be used to scent custards – rinse and dry after use. Each pod can be used several times.

Nuts and Seeds
These are a delicious addition to salads, stir-fries, desserts, etc., and can be dry roasted for extra flavour before sprinkling over dishes. When buying sesame seeds buy the unhulled variety; these are a rich source of calcium, and the sesame seed paste, tahini, is useful for the store cupboard.

Bran and Cereal Germs

Wheat, oat or soya bran for extra fibre – and wheat or oat germ containing valuable vitamin E – can be added to breakfast dishes if desired. They are relatively starch-free and are regarded as neutral. Wheat germ should be bought in small quantities and as fresh as possible; store it in a cool place as it can go rancid very quickly. 'Stabilized' wheat germ is sometimes a better buy.

Pulses

Pulses and legumes are not usually recommended for the Hay system because they contain too high a proportion of both protein and starch to be compatible in themselves, and can cause digestive problems in people who are not accustomed to them. Vegetarians can build up a tolerance for them and, combined in the way we suggest in the Recipes section, can find them a useful addition to their diet.

Equipment

Good basic kitchen equipment will make all the difference to the ease and speed with which you can prepare Hay meals. Some of it is expensive but most items will last a lifetime.

- If possible buy stainless steel saucepans in preference to aluminium which may be one of the factors implicated in the cause of Alzheimer's disease
- Heavy cast-iron frying pans are best for omelettes. Two such pans, one with a 20-cm/8-in diameter and the other with a 25-cm/10-in diameter, would be ideal. The larger one can be used for stir-frying vegetables if you do not possess a wok, but this, too, would be a useful addition to your kitchen
- A good chopping board, a set of good kitchen knives and good kitchen scissors are essential, likewise a salad spinner and a reliable set of weighing scales
- In the Hay kitchen, vegetables are cooked as little as possible to preserve the essential vitamins and flavour. For this a steamer, preferably with two or three tiers, gives the best results
- For speed, an electric hand whisk, a blender and a food processor will pay dividends in time saved in food preparation
- An enamelled cast-iron casserole is useful for many dishes which can be started on the top of the cooker and then transferred to the oven to finish. Another useful piece of equipment is a slow cooker; so many casserole dishes can be prepared in advance and left to cook gently until needed, a bonus when entertaining and the guests are late!

Notes on Terms, Quantities, Oven Temperatures and Freezing

Most recipes serve four unless otherwise stated. They are designed to be flexible so that they can easily be scaled down or up as needed.

Quantities are given in metric, imperial and US cup measurements. Do not try to interchange them – for best results use one set of measurements rather than a combination. The American terms for ingredients and equipment, where these differ from the UK ones, are given throughout.

Spoon measures given are level unless stated otherwise.

Oven temperatures are given in Centigrade, Fahrenheit and Gas Mark. Oven efficiency varies enormously so you may need to make adjustments to suit your oven.

Because many of the recipes are low in fat, or use raw or only lightly cooked vegetables, they are not suitable for freezing; where a dish will freeze well this has been specified.

TABLE OF COMPATIBLE FOODS

Columns I and III are incompatible (see note below right)

I FOR PROTEIN MEALS

Proteins

Meat of all kinds: Beef, lamb, pork, venison

Poultry: Chicken, duck, goose, turkey

Game: Pheasant, partridge, grouse, hare

Fish of all kinds including shellfish

Eggs

Cheese

Milk: cow, goat or sheep, but not UHT or homogenized, also unsweetened soya milk (all milks combine best with fruit and should not be served at a meat meal)

Yoghurt, including soya yoghurt

Quark, Fromage Frais

Fruits

Apples

Apricots (fresh & dried)

Blackberries

Blueberries

Cherries

Clementines

Currants (black, red or white if ripe)

Gooseberries (if ripe)

Grapefruit

Grapes (black and white)

Guavas

Kiwis

Lemons

Limes

Loganberries

Lychees

Mangoes

Melons (eaten alone as a fruit meal)

Nectarines

Oranges

Papayas (Pawpaw)

Passion Fruit

Peaches

Pears

Pineapple

Prunes (for occasional use)

Raspberries

Satsumas

Strawberries

Tangerines*

II NEUTRAL FOODS

Can be combined with either Col I or Col III

Nuts & Seeds

All except peanuts

Nut & seed butters (not peanut butter)

Fats

Butter

Cream

Crème fraîche

Cream cheese

Egg yolks

Olive oil

Sunflower seed oil (cold pressed)

Sesame seed oil (cold pressed)

Walnut oil (cold pressed)

Bran

Wheat, oat or soya bran

Wheatgerm

Vegetables

All green and root vegetables (except potatoes and Jerusalem artichokes)

Asparagus

Aubergines (eggplants)

Beans (all fresh green beans)

Beetroot (Beet)

Broccoli

Brussels sprouts

Cabbage

Calabrese

Carrots

Cauliflower

Celery

Celeriac

Chard

Courgettes (zucchini)

Globe artichokes

Kohlrabi

Leeks

Marrow (squash)

Mushrooms

Onions

Parsnips

Peas

Spinach

Swedes (rutabagas)

Turnips

III FOR STARCH MEALS

Cereals

Wholegrain: wheat, barley, maize (corn), oats, millet rice (brown, unpolished), rye, buckwheat, quinoa

Bread 100% wholewheat

Flour 100% or 85%

Oatmeal or flakes

Wholewheat egg-free pastas

Milk: cow, goat or sheep, but not UHT or homogenized, nor soya milk – in strict moderation only

Yoghurt (not soya yoghurt) – in moderation

Sweet Fruits

Bananas – ripe

Plaintain

Dates (fresh & dried)

Figs (fresh & dried)

Grapes – extra sweet

Papaya if very ripe

Pears if very sweet & ripe

Currants

Raisins

Sultanas

Vegetables

Corn & Sweetcorn

Potatoes

Jerusalem Artichokes

Pumpkin

Winter Squashes

Sweet Potato

*NB Cranberries, plums and rhubarb and not recommended

I FOR PROTEIN MEALS

Salad Dressings
French dressing made with oil
and lemon juice or apple
cider vinegar
Cream dressing
Mayonnaise (homemade)

Sugar Substitute
Diluted frozen orange juice
Concentrated fruit juices

Soya Products
(use in moderation unless on
a vegetarian diet)
Soya beans and all soya
products including TVP*
Tofu (not smoked)
Other plant proteins: Quorn

*NB all soya products are
processed: use sparingly

II NEUTRAL FOODS

Can be combined with
either Col I or Col III

Saladings
Avocados
Chicory (endive)
Corn salad (mâche)
Cucumber
Fennel
Garlic
Lettuce
Mustard & cress
Olives (in brine)
Peppers red & green
Radishes
Spring Onions (scallions)
Sprouted legumes
Sprouted seeds
Tomatoes (uncooked)
Watercress

Herbs and Flavourings
All herbs fresh or dried
Vegetable stock (bouillon)
cubes and powders
All spices – use sparingly
Yeast extract
Miso/tamari/shoyu
Grated lemon rind (organic)
Grated orange rind (organic)
Vanilla pod/extract

Sugar Substitute
Raisins and raisin juice
Currants
Sultanas
Honey, Maple syrup (in strict
moderation)

III FOR STARCH MEALS

Salad Dressings
Sweet or soured cream
Olive oil or cold pressed seed
oils
Fresh tomato juice with oil
and seasoning

Sugars
(All sugar in strict moderation)
Honey, Maple syrup
Molasses

Pulses/Legumes**
Aduki beans
Black-eyed beans
Butterbeans
Cannellini beans
Chick peas (Garbanzos)
Haricot beans
Lentils – all kinds
Marrow fat peas
Peanuts
Pinto beans
Red kidney beans

**Pulses and legumes are not recommended for the Hay System as they combine too high a proportion of both protein and starch which impedes digestion (see full explanation in *Food Combining for Health*). However, vegetarians may use them combined with vegetables and salads.

NB These tables should be used only for checking the compatibility of foods and ingredients i.e. to make sure you do not mix foods that fight. They bear no relation to Dr Hay's concept of acid/alkali *forming* foods and their balance which is explained on pages 1–2.

DRINK COMBINATION TABLE

Reproduced from *Food Combining for Vegetarians* – Jackie Le Tissier, Thorsons 1992

I FOR PROTEIN MEALS

Coffee/tea – strict moderation
 – no sugar – milk*
Non-cereal coffee substitutes
Lemon teas – unsweetened
Fruit teas – unsweetened
Fruit juices –
 fresh/bottled/vacuum
 packed – unsweetened
Grape juice – if not too sweet
Tomato juice –
 cooked/tinned/vacuum
 packed
Milk –
 cow's/goat's/sheep's/soya*
Lassis – made with protein
 fruits only – unsweetened

II NEUTRAL FOODS

Water – tap/bottled
Dandelion coffee
Herb teas
Tomato juice – fresh
Vegetable juices –
 fresh/cooked/vacuum
 packed/bottled – non-starch
 only
Instant
 vegetable/bouillon/yeast
 extract drinks

III FOR STARCH MEALS

Coffee/tea – strict moderation
 – sugar & milk*
Cereal coffee substitutes
Chocolate/cocoa* – made
 with water/cream or very
 diluted milk
Grape juice – only if very
 sweet
Carob drinks – sugar* made
 with water/cream or very
 diluted milk

*Use very sparingly

ALCOHOLIC DRINKS

All in strict moderation:
Wines – dry
Cider – dry
Liqueurs – dry

All in strict moderation:
Gin
Rum
Vodka
Whisky
Brandy

All in strict moderation:
Beer
Lager
Ale
Stout
Wine – sweet
Liqueurs – sweet
Sake

Recipes for Alkaline Meals

All recipes are suitable for vegetarians

This section contains recipes for dishes comprising only alkaline forming foods. All the recipes that follow are compatible with each other.

It is suggested that one meal a day should be chosen from this group, and many people find that breakfast is the easiest time to fit this important alkaline meal into their daily meal plan.

Dr Hay considered that breakfast was a superfluous meal, but for most people a light breakfast of fruit (perhaps with milk or yoghurt) makes an ideal start to the day. People who prefer a more substantial meal will find suggestions in the Protein and Starch sections; an alkaline meal (such as soup, salad, vegetable dish and dessert) can then be taken at midday or in the evening.

Note Although many alkaline foods are neutral and can be combined with all foods, others are not. This applies particularly to fruit, which though alkaline-forming should only be eaten with compatible food groups, i.e. acid and sub-acid fruits with alkaline foods or proteins, and sweet fruits with starches. Please refer to the Table of Compatible Foods on page 20 if ever in doubt.

Food and Drinks that Can Be Combined for an Alkaline Meal

Dairy Products

Milk, yoghurt, buttermilk, quark, fromage frais (1% and 8%), cream cheese, cream, crème fraîche

Vegetables

All green and root vegetables except potatoes, sweet potatoes (yams) and Jerusalem artichokes.
Uncooked tomatoes
All salad greens and herbs

Acid Fruits

(see comprehensive list in Table of Compatible Foods, page 20)

Apples, apricots (fresh and dried), cherries, pears, pineapples, grapes, grapefruit, lemons, oranges, peaches, nectarines, tangerines, satsumas, strawberries, raspberries and berries of all kinds.

Note Mushrooms, nuts, oils, raisins, cream cheese, butter, cream, soured cream and egg yolks combine with all meals. Milk and yoghurt and other milk products are not *concentrated* proteins and combine best with fruit and vegetables.

Drinks

Weak tea, filter coffee (though not recommended), dandelion coffee, herb teas

Soft drinks: fresh tomato juice, apple juice, grape juice, fresh orange juice, fresh lemon or lime juice with water, fresh unsweetened grapefruit juice.

Spring water

Alcoholic drinks or carbonated waters are not recommended with an alkaline meal

Citrus Fruit and Apple Serves 2

A sharp and refreshing combination of flavours complemented by the warm flavour of cinnamon

2 cups/350g/12 oz red dessert apples, peeled and roughly chopped
⅓ cup/4 tbsps freshly squeezed lemon juice
⅓ cup/4 tbsps freshly squeezed orange juice
¼–½ tsp ground (powdered) cinnamon
honey or maple syrup to taste (optional)

1 Place the apple, lemon and orange juice in a food processor or blender, and blend to a smooth purée.
2 Stir in the cinnamon to taste, sweeten with a little honey or maple syrup if desired, then chill for 2–3 hours before serving.

Serve as a breakfast dish, or as a dessert topped with yoghurt, cream or ice-cream.

Variation:
Rather than purée the fruit mixture, you can just toss the apples in the lemon, orange juice and cinnamon and serve at once.

Melon Crush Makes 570ml/1 pt (US 2½ cups)

For those who do not favour a substantial breakfast, this drink gets the day off to a good start

1 x 675g/1½ lb Melon (Galia melons are
    particularly delicious for this recipe,
    but other varieties are also suitable –
    make sure your melon is very ripe)

1   Halve the melon and remove the seeds.
2   Scoop out the flesh, place in a food processor or blender, then blend until smooth and creamy. Chill. We drink the juice like this, but if you prefer a thinner drink add a little water to adjust the consistency.

Variation:
Add a sprinkling of ground (powdered) ginger for a 'sharper' flavour.

Note:
Melon should always be eaten alone as a single meal, so do not combine this drink with any other foods.

Pineapple, Apricot and Sultana (Golden Seedless Raisin) Muesli (Granola) Makes 450g/1lb (US 3 cups)

⅔ cup/75g/3 oz dried pineapple, cut into small pieces

½ cup/75g/3 oz dried apricots, cut into small pieces

⅓ cup/50g/2 oz sultanas (golden seedless raisins)

½ cup/50g/2 oz pumpkin seeds, finely chopped

¼ cup/25g/1 oz pine kernels

¼ cup/25g/1 oz nibbed almonds

½ cup/50g/2 oz sunflower seeds

⅓ cup/50g/2 oz sesame seeds

1   Mix altogether and store in an airtight container.

Serve with the fruit juice of your choice, or with boiling water or diluted cream.

Toasted Millet and Sultana (Golden Seedless Raisin) Porridge Serves 2

2 tsp olive or sunflower oil
½ cup/100g/4 oz millet
2½ cups/570ml/1 pt boiling spring water

⅔ cup/100g/4 oz sultanas (golden
  seedless raisins)

1   Heat the oil in a large pan and toast the millet grains until golden brown.
2   Remove the pan from the heat and slowly add the water.
3   Stir in the sultanas (golden seedless raisins) then cover and simmer gently for 20–30 minutes or until the millet is swollen and fluffy.

For a very porridgy alternative, simmer the millet gently for a few extra minutes, stirring occasionally, until the mixture becomes very sticky – our favourite way of eating it!

Note:
Millet is the only alkaline grain.

Muesli (Granola) Serves 1

Muesli (granola) is now a very popular breakfast dish, but unfortunately the commercial muesli mix bears no relationship at all to the original raw fruit porridge devised by Dr Max Bircher-Benner for his patients. Modern mueslis are essentially starchy cereal mixes, whereas in Dr Bircher-Benner's muesli, grated raw apple and/or other acid fruit predominated and only a level tablespoonful of fresh rolled oats or medium oatmeal was permitted. Because the cereal content is so small and also because it is raw, freshly made muesli, prepared according to Dr Bircher-Benner's recipe, may be regarded as an alkaline meal, and the recipe is given below. However, if you prefer a mixed cereal dish this is not muesli and should be regarded as a starch meal

Dr Bircher-Benner's Muesli
1 tbsp rolled oats or medium oatmeal
¼ cup/3 tbsps spring water
1 tbsp freshly squeezed lemon juice

¼ cup/3 tbsps whole milk or plain
  yoghurt
1 large or 2 small dessert apples
1 tbsp grated almonds or hazelnuts

1 Soak the oats or oatmeal with the water overnight.
2 In the morning, add the lemon juice and milk or yoghurt. Grate (shred) the well-scrubbed apples into the mixture and sprinkle the grated nuts on top.
3 Serve at once.

Additional Alkaline Breakfast Suggestions

- Cooking (baking) apple stuffed with raisins, cinnamon and toasted, chopped hazelnuts or sunflower seeds, then baked and served with cream/diluted cream
- Stewed apple sprinkled with cinnamon and ginger
- Fruit – any fruit as listed on page 20, Column 1
- Melon eaten alone
- Freshly squeezed fruit juice
- Fresh tomato juice
- Fresh vegetable or salad juices
- Fresh grapefruit and orange segments
- Sliced dessert apple with raisins and yoghurt
- Soaked Hunza apricots with a little wheatgerm and yoghurt (bran – either wheat, oat or soya – and wheatgerm are regarded as neutral and may therefore be added to suitable breakfast dishes if desired)

Cream of Leek Soup Serves 4

2 tbsps/25g/1 oz unsalted (sweet) butter
2 large leeks, sliced
1 medium parsnip, chopped
1 medium carrot, chopped

5 cups/1 L/2 pt spring water
sea salt and freshly ground black pepper
⅔ cup/150ml/¼ pt single (light) cream

1 Melt the unsalted butter in a thick-based pan and add the vegetables. Sauté for a few minutes, stirring to prevent sticking.
2 Add the water and bring to the boil. Reduce the heat, cover and simmer for 15–20 minutes or until the vegetables are tender.
3 Allow to cool slightly, then blend in a blender or food processor.
4 Return to the pan and season to taste. Stir in the cream and reheat gently without boiling.

Freezing:
Can be frozen, but add the cream when reheating to serve.

End of Winter Soup Serves 4–6

This is a useful standby soup that can be made in quantity and stored in the refrigerator for several days. The proportion of vegetables one to the other is really a matter of taste, and not critical

1 tbsp olive oil
1 large onion, chopped
1 swede (rutabaga), roughly chopped
½ small firm cabbage, shredded

5 cups/1 L/2 pt spring water
freshly grated nutmeg
sea salt and freshly ground black pepper
soured cream to garnish

1   Heat the oil in a thick-based pan, add the onion and stir until transparent.
2   Add the remaining vegetables and the water and bring to the boil. Cover and simmer gently until the vegetables are soft, about 25–30 minutes.
3   Allow to cool a little, add nutmeg and transfer to a food processor or blender. Blend to a thick purée.
4   Return to the pan and season, adding a little more spring water if the soup is too thick.
5   Reheat gently and serve with a swirl of soured cream on top of each portion.

Spicy Fennel, Leek and Red Pepper Soup Serves 4

1½ tbsps olive or sunflower oil
1 lb/450g fennel, cleaned weight, finely
    chopped
1 lb/450g leeks, cleaned weight, finely
    chopped
2 cups/225g/8 oz red pepper, deseeded
    and finely diced

2 tsp five spice powder
1 vegetable stock (bouillon) cube
1¼ cups/285ml/½ pt boiling spring water
2 cups/425ml/¾ pt apple juice
⅓ cup/4 tbsps single (light) cream
sea salt and freshly ground black pepper

1 Heat the oil in a large pan. Cook the fennel, leeks and red pepper with
   the spice, covered and over a gentle heat, for 15 minutes or until
   tender.
2 Dissolve the stock (bouillon) cube in the water and add to the
   vegetables.
3 Stir in the apple juice, bring to the boil and simmer, covered,
   for 15 minutes.
4 Dilute the cream to 150ml/¼ pt (US ⅔ cup) water, and add to the soup.
   Reheat gently, season and serve.

Note:
Five-spice powder is a Chinese mixture of spices such as anise peppers,
star anise, cinnamon, cloves and fennel. It is available in speciality food
shops and some large supermarkets.

Freezing:
Can be frozen.

Parsnip and Apple Soup Serves 4–6

2 tbsps/25g/1 oz unsalted (sweet) butter
2 shallots or 1 medium onion, chopped
2 medium parsnips, chopped
1 medium baking apple, peeled and
   chopped

5 cups/1 L/2 pt spring water or vegetable
   stock (bouillon)
2 tbsps chopped fresh parsley
⅔ cup/150ml/¼ pt single (light) cream
sea salt and freshly ground black pepper

1   Melt the unsalted butter in a large pan.
2   Add the chopped vegetables and apple and sauté, stirring frequently,
    until the shallot or onion is transparent.
3   Add the water or stock (bouillon), bring to the boil and reduce heat.
    Cover and simmer for 30 minutes. Leave to cool slightly.
4   Blend in a blender or food processor.
5   Add the parsley and reheat to just below boiling point. Remove from
    the heat, stir in the cream, season to taste and serve.

Freezing:
Can be frozen but add the parsley and cream when reheating to serve.

Savoury Lettuce Soup Serves 6

Lettuce is often ignored as an ingredient other than for salads, and this soup is a fine example of how versatile it can be

2 tbsps olive or sunflower oil
3 cups/350g/12 oz onions, finely chopped
2 cups/225g/8 oz celery, finely chopped
10 oz/275g lettuce (we find the firm
   Iceberg variety the best to use), very
   finely shredded then chopped

1 vegetable stock (bouillon) cube
2½ tbsps tamari
1 tsp freshly grated nutmeg
3¾ cups/850ml/1½ pt spring water
sea salt and freshly ground black pepper

1 Heat the oil in a large pan. Add the onion and celery, cover and cook covered for 15–20 minutes, or until soft.
2 Add the lettuce and cook covered for a further 5 minutes.
3 Mix in the stock (bouillon) cube, tamari and nutmeg, then add the water.
4 Bring to the boil, season and simmer a further 5 minutes.

This can be served as above or blended to make a smooth soup.

Freezing:
Can be frozen.

Apple and Avocado Salad Serves 4

This salad needs to be assembled quickly and served immediately to prevent discoloration

2 dessert apples, peeled and diced
1/3 cup/50g/2 oz sun-dried raisins
1/3 cup/50g/2 oz hazelnuts, chopped

1 stalk celery, chopped
Yoghurt Dressing (page 47)
2 avocados, halved and peeled

1 Toss the first four ingredients lightly with enough yoghurt dressing to moisten them.
2 Fill the avocado halves with the mixture arrange and serve at once.

Courgette (Zucchini) and Carrot Salad Serves 4–6

Small spring carrots and the early baby courgettes (zucchini) are best for this salad

⅓ cup/50g/2 oz dried apricots, soaked in spring water overnight
⅓ cup/50g/2 oz sun-dried raisins
2 cups/225g/8 oz carrots, thinly sliced
2 cups/225g/8 oz courgettes (zucchini), thinly sliced

⅓ cup /4 tbsps sunflower seeds
⅓ cup/90ml/3 fl oz freshly squeezed orange juice
⅔ cup/150ml/¼ pt French Dressing (page 45)
sea salt and freshly ground black pepper

1 Drain and chop the apricots and combine with the raisins.
2 Mix together the carrots, courgettes (zucchini), dried fruit and sunflower seeds.
3 Add the orange juice to the French dressing and mix thoroughly with the salad.
4 Season to taste if necessary.

Note:
The quantity of dressing needed may vary according to taste.

Salad à la Guacamole Serves 4

2 ripe avocados
4 tomatoes, skinned and roughly
   chopped

½ cucumber, peeled and roughly chopped
2 stalks celery, finely chopped
½ small onion or 1 shallot, grated

Dressing
juice of 1 lime
⅓ cup/4 tbsps olive oil
sea salt and freshly ground black pepper

1 Peel the avocados, remove the stones and slice the flesh.
2 Place in a bowl with the tomatoes, cucumber, celery and onion.
3 Combine the lime juice, olive oil and seasoning to make a dressing.
4 Toss the salad gently with the dressing, test for seasoning and serve.

Fresh Pineapple Salad Serves 4

The colour and flavour contrast in this salad make the cost well worth it!

½ lollo rosso or red oak leaf lettuce
½ large pineapple
1 avocado

¼ cup/25g/1 oz pine kernels
French Dressing (page 45)
sea salt and freshly ground black pepper

1   Wash and dry the lettuce and tear the leaves into smaller pieces.
2   Remove the outer skin from the pineapple and cut the flesh into bite-sized pieces.
3   Halve the avocado, remove the stone and then peel and slice the flesh.
4   Mix all the ingredients together with sufficient French dressing to moisten.
5   Add extra seasoning only if necessary.

Winter Crunch Salad Serves 4

1 cup/100g/4 oz parsnip, coarsely grated (shredded)

1 cup/100g/4 oz carrots, coarsely grated (shredded)

1 cup/100g/4 oz swede (rutabaga), coarsely grated (shredded)

1 shallot or ½ small onion, chopped

⅔ cup/150ml/¼ pt soured cream

1 tsp coarse grain mustard

2 tsp clear honey

sea salt and freshly ground black pepper

1 Mix together all the prepared vegetables
2 Combine the soured cream, mustard and honey and add to the vegetables.
3 Season to taste and if possible leave for 30 minutes or so before serving.

Winter Beet Salad Serves 4–6

2 cups/225g/8 oz carrots, coarsely grated (shredded)
2 cups/225g/8 oz raw beetroot, coarsely grated (shredded)
¼ cup/25g/1 oz onion or shallot, grated (shredded)

2 tbsps chopped fresh mint
⅔ cup/150ml/¼ pt plain yoghurt
1 tbsp clear honey
1 tbsp freshly squeezed lemon juice
sea salt and freshly ground black pepper

1 Mix together the prepared vegetables and chopped mint.
2 Combine the yoghurt with the honey and lemon juice and season to taste.
3 Toss the vegetables with the yoghurt dressing and place in a serving dish.
4 If possible, allow the flavours to blend for a few hours before serving.

Orange and Herb Dressing Serves 4

A very herby dressing with a delicious flavour

1½ tbsps olive or sunflower oil
⅓ cup/4 tbsps spring water
2 tsp grated organic rind
1½ tbsps finely chopped fresh parsley

1½ tbsps finely chopped fresh mint
    or ¾ tbsp dried mint
1½ tbsps finely chopped fresh chives
sea salt and freshly ground black pepper

1   Mix all the ingredients together then refrigerate for 1 hour to allow the
    flavours to blend.

French Dressing Makes 150ml/¼ pt (US ⅔ cup)

½ tsp sea salt
1 clove garlic, crushed (optional)
pinch paprika
2 tbsps freshly squeezed lemon juice

freshly ground black pepper
½ cup/6 tbsps extra virgin olive oil or
cold-pressed sunflower seed oil

1   Put all the ingredients into a screw-topped jar and shake vigorously.

This amount should be enough to dress two salads or more and can be stored in the refrigerator for a few days.

Variation:
If you prefer a sweeter dressing, a teaspoon of clear honey can be added to the basic recipe. Chopped chives or a little chopped shallot may be substituted for the garlic.

Fast Mayonnaise Makes about 285ml/½ pt (US 1¼ cups)

2 egg yolks at room temperature
1 tsp dry mustard
pinch sea salt
freshly ground black pepper

1 tbsp freshly squeezed lemon juice
1¼ cups/285ml/½ pt extra virgin olive oil
1 tbsp boiling spring water

1 Put the egg yolks, mustard and seasoning into a blender.
2 Add the lemon juice and blend the ingredients together at the lowest speed.
3 Remove the centre cap of the blender goblet and, with the motor running at lowest speed, pour the oil on to the egg mixture *very slowly* – almost drop by drop.
4 Continue to add the oil very slowly until the mixture begins to thicken.
5 Add the rest of the oil in a steady stream and lastly add the boiling water. Switch off the blender.

This mayonnaise will keep in the refrigerator if well covered.

Variation:
For an interesting variation, the addition of a couple of tablespoons of chopped green herbs such as parsley, sorrel, chives or young spinach leaves, after the mayonnaise has thickened, will transform it into a *sauce verte;* this can be used as a salad dressing or as an accompaniment to cold trout, salmon or chicken.

Yoghurt Dressing Makes about 150ml/¼ pt (US ⅔ cup)

This is a quickly made dressing – delicious on grated (shredded) root
vegetable salads

2 tsps freshly squeezed lemon juice
sea salt and freshly ground black pepper
⅔ cup/150ml/¼ pt plain yoghurt

mixed fresh herbs of choice, finely
chopped

1   Mix the lemon juice with the sea salt and pepper. Stir in the yoghurt
    and chopped herbs and pour over the prepared salad.

This dressing can be varied by the use of different herbs: chopped winter
savory enhances a salad of green beans; tarragon, thyme or oregano lift
most root vegetable salads; a few chopped chives or finely chopped
shallot give an extra bite to the flavour.

Stuffed Baby Marrow (Summer Squash)

Serves 4 as a main course

A delicious savoury way to top slices of marrow

4 slices baby marrow (summer squash) or
    large courgette (zucchini),
    approximately 4 cm/1½ in thick by
    7½ cm/3 in diameter
2 tbsps olive or sunflower oil
1½ cups/175g/6 oz onions, finely
    chopped
1½ cups/175g/6 oz red pepper, deseeded
    and finely diced
2 cloves garlic, crushed

½ vegetable stock (bouillon) cube
3 cups/175g/6 oz mushrooms, very finely
    chopped
2 tsp tamari
1 tbsp finely chopped fresh thyme
    or ½ tbsp dried thyme
1 cup/100g/4 oz ground sunflower seeds
¼ cup/25g/1 oz whole sunflower seeds
sea salt and freshly ground black pepper

1   Preheat the oven to 200°C/400°F/Gas Mark 6.
2   Scoop out the middle of the marrow (summer squash) or courgette (zucchini) slices, leaving a thin ring.
3   Heat the oil and fry the onion and red pepper until soft. Add the garlic and stock (bouillon) cube and combine, then add the mushrooms, tamari and thyme and cook for a further minute.
4   Take the pan off the heat and stir in the ground and whole sunflower seeds to form a moist but stiff mixture, adding more ground seeds if necessary. Season to taste.
5   Place the rings on a lightly greased baking sheet and fill with the stuffing.
6   Cover with foil and bake for 30–40 minutes, or until the skins are tender.

The stuffing mix can also be used to fill peppers or large mushrooms.

Caraway Stuffed Aubergine (Eggplant) Serves 4

A lovely way to serve this vegetable

2 aubergines (eggplants), approximately
    350g/12 oz each in weight
2 tbsps olive or sunflower oil
2 cups/225g/8 oz onions, finely chopped
2 cups/225g/8 oz red pepper, deseeded
    and finely chopped

4 cups/225g/8 oz button mushrooms,
    thinly sliced
1½ tbsps caraway seeds, lightly toasted
    then roughly chopped or ground in a
    pestle and mortar
sea salt and freshly ground black pepper

1 Preheat the oven to 190°C/375°F/Gas Mark 5.
2 Remove the stalks from the aubergines (eggplants), then place in a
   saucepan half filled with water.
3 Bring to the boil, simmer for approximately 10 minutes or until tender,
   then remove and put to one side to cool.
4 Heat the oil and fry the onion until soft. Add the red pepper, cook for
   2–3 minutes, then add the mushrooms and caraway seeds and cook
   for a further minute.
5 Halve the aubergines (eggplants) and carefully scoop out the flesh,
   leaving the shells intact. Chop the scooped out flesh, add to the
   vegetable mix, combine well and season.
6 Pile the mixture into the prepared shells, cover with foil and bake on a
   lightly greased baking sheet for 25 minutes, or until well heated
   through.

Cucumber and Yoghurt Mushrooms Serves 2

A delicious mixture of flavours – light and refreshing

1 tbsp olive or sunflower oil
1½ cups/175g/6 oz cucumber
3 cups/175g/6 oz button mushrooms,
 halved or quartered
pinch paprika

¼ cup/3 tbsps plain yoghurt
1–2 tbsps freshly squeezed lemon juice
sea salt and freshly ground black pepper
toasted nori flakes (optional)

1 Score the skin of the cucumber with a fork so that it softens on cooking (it also produces an attractive appearance!) then cut into small dice.
2 Heat the oil and gently fry the cucumber until tender.
3 Add the mushrooms and paprika and cook for a further 3–4 minutes.
4 Remove the pan from the heat, stir in the yoghurt and lemon juice to taste, then season.
5 Sprinkle with toasted nori flakes if desired.

Serve on starch-free crackers, or on slices of tomato. Ideal as a light lunch or evening meal, or for a quick main course.

Variation:
Alternatively, grill (broil) or bake aubergine (eggplant) slices until tender, pile the cucumber, mushroom and yoghurt mix on top and heat through.

Note:
Nori flakes are a dried sea vegetable, available in good health food shops.

Courgette (Zucchini) and Carrot Wheels Serves 4

This vegetable dish with its vivid green and orange colouring will brighten any meal

4 courgettes (zucchini), 100g/4 oz each in weight (for stuffing, so select plump ones as opposed to long and thin!)
2 tbsps olive or sunflower oil
1 cup/100g/4 oz onions, finely chopped

4 cups/450g/1 lb carrots, finely chopped
1 vegetable stock (bouillon) cube
1½ tbsps finely chopped fresh thyme or ¾ tbsp dried thyme
sea salt and freshly ground black pepper

1   Preheat the oven to 190°C/375°F/Gas Mark 5.
2   Top and tail the courgettes (zucchini) then slice in half lengthways. Use a melon baller or teaspoon to scoop out the middle, leaving a thin layer of flesh on the surface of the skin.
3   Steam the skins until tender but still maintaining their shape. Cool.
4   Finely chop the scooped out courgette (zucchini) flesh.
5   Heat the oil, add the onion and carrot and cook, covered, for 10 minutes. Add the chopped courgette (zucchini), mix in the stock (bouillon) cube and thyme and cook for a further minute.
6   Season, then place the mixture in a food processor or blender and blend until smooth.
7   Place four courgette (zucchini) halves onto a lightly greased baking sheet and divide the carrot mixture between each, piling it into the skins. Smooth over to form a mound.
8   Top each mound with a remaining courgette (zucchini) half to form a sausage shape, then gently turn these on to their sides.
9   Cover with foil and bake for 20 minutes. Cut each courgette (zucchini) into four, producing a wheel effect, or serve whole as prepared.

Serve garnished with some extra chopped fresh thyme if available. This vegetable dish also makes an unusual main course.

Braised Lettuce and Onion with Ginger and Nutmeg Serves 4

Lettuce is often forgotten as a side vegetable, but it is delicious when combined with other ingredients as in this dish

2 tbsps olive or sunflower oil
1 lb/450g onions, thinly sliced
1¼ lb/550g firm lettuce (we use Iceberg), very thinly shredded
1 tsp freshly grated nutmeg

¼ cup/3 tbsps grated fresh root ginger (discard the fibres)
sea salt and freshly ground black pepper
2 tbsps/25g/1 oz butter

1 Preheat the oven to 190°C/375°F/Gas Mark 5.
2 Heat the oil and cook the onion, covered, until soft. Add the lettuce and cook for a further 5 minutes.
3 Mix in the nutmeg and ginger juice and season to taste.
4 Place the mixture in an ovenproof dish, dot butter on top, then cover and bake/braise for 15–20 minutes.

Parsnip and Swede (Rutabaga) Bake Serves 4–6

A delicious, sweet vegetable mixture, delicately flavoured with caraway

1 lb/450g swede (rutabaga), roughly
  chopped
1 lb/450g parsnips, roughly chopped
1¼ cups/285ml/½ pt spring water
1 clove garlic, crushed

1½ tbsps caraway seeds, lightly toasted
  then finely chopped or crushed in a
  pestle and mortar
sea salt and freshly ground black pepper

1 Preheat the oven to 200°C/400°F/Gas Mark 6.
2 Place the swede (rutabaga) and parsnip in a saucepan and add the
   water.
3 Bring to the boil, cover and simmer until tender, adding more water if
   necessary.
4 Once cooked, drain and then mash until smooth.
5 Stir in the garlic and caraway seeds and season. Spoon into an oven
   proof dish. Smooth over and bake for 20–30 minutes uncovered.

Serve as a vegetable accompaniment, or sprinkle with chopped nuts for a
main course dish. Can also be shaped into balls and baked. Alternatively,
heat through in a saucepan and serve as a vegetable purée.

Desserts

Probably the best finish for an alkaline meal is any fresh fruit in season. If preferred it can be sliced and served with yoghurt, cream, fromage frais or junket. Choose from any of the fruits listed in Column 1 of the Table of Compatible Foods (page 20).

Classic combinations such as strawberries or raspberries with cream, and sliced peaches or nectarines with Greek yoghurt or cream, are ideal. An autumn favourite is blackberry and apple lightly stewed with a little honey and served with Greek yoghurt. Delicious fruit fools (parfaits) can be made by stirring purées of fresh and lightly cooked fruits into a mix of half yoghurt and half whipped cream. Fruit can also be served with a topping of nuts, especially almonds, or seeds.

Pineapple Islands Serves 4

8 slices fresh pineapple
1¼ cups/285ml/½ pt freshly squeezed
   orange juice

½ cup/50g/2 oz flaked (slivered) almonds
crème fraîche (optional)

1 Place the pineapple slices in a shallow dish and pour the orange juice over them. Chill for 1–2 hours in the refrigerator.
2 Divide between 4 individual serving dishes.
3 Toast the flaked (slivered) almonds lightly under a hot grill (broiler) and scatter over the pineapple.
4 Serve at once with crème fraîche if liked.

Devonshire Junket Serves 4–6

2½ cups/570ml/1 pt Channel Island (full-cream) milk
1 tbsp clear honey
1–2 tbsps rum or brandy, according to taste

1 tsp vegetarian rennet
a little freshly grated nutmeg
clotted cream or crème fraîche

1   Bring the milk to blood heat (37.4°C/98.4°F), using a dairy thermometer if you are not used to judging this.
2   Mix the honey with the rum or brandy in a serving bowl and place in a corner of the kitchen where it can be left undisturbed.
3   Pour the warmed milk into the bowl, stirring as you go.
4   Stir in the rennet gently and leave to set.
5   When set, sprinkle the surface with nutmeg and serve with clotted cream or crème fraîche.

As an alternative to the usual cream or yoghurt, this traditional recipe makes an unusual and delicious accompaniment to fruit.

Raspberry and Redcurrant Mousse Serves 4

2 cups/225g/8 oz redcurrants, stringed
2 tbsps apple juice
1 lb/450g ripe raspberries

2 tbsps mild clear honey
1¼ cups/285ml/½ pt double (heavy) cream

1   Place the redcurrants and apple juice in a saucepan and gently heat through until the juice begins to run.
2   Combine the raspberries, redcurrants and honey in a blender or food processor and blend to a purée.
3   Whip the cream and fold into the purée to give a marbled effect.
4   Spoon into serving glasses and chill until needed.

This recipe can easily be adapted for any fresh fruit; blackcurrants make a particularly delicious mousse.

Freezing:
When cream is used fruit mousses will freeze well; however if a lighter dessert is required the fruit purée can be combined with Greek yoghurt, but this does not freeze successfully unless you have an ice-cream maker.

Baked Apples with Fresh Ginger Serves 4

4 large dessert apples
⅓ cup/50g/2 oz large seeded raisins
½ cup/125ml/4 fl oz spring water

1 tsp grated fresh ginger
⅓ cup/4 tbsps apple juice

1 Preheat the oven to 180°C/350°F/Gas Mark 4.
2 Core the apples, leaving a larger opening at one end of each apple for the filling, and place in a buttered ovenproof dish.
3 Heat the raisins with the water in a small saucepan until soft and mushy and all the water has been absorbed.
4 Remove from the heat and mix in the grated ginger.
5 Spoon the raisin mixture into the centre of each apple, pushing it down well.
6 Pour a tablespoon of apple juice over each apple and bake in the lower part of the oven for 20–30 minutes, until softened but still fairly firm.

Serve with 8% fromage frais or Greek yoghurt.

Quince Cream Serves 4

A delicious and unusual autumn treat. This large, pear-shaped fruit was common in eighteenth-century England and cookbooks of the period have many recipes for using quinces. This one is adapted from *The Art of Cookery made Plain and Easy* by Mrs Hannah Glasse. If you see quinces for sale or have a friend who has a tree, do seize the opportunity to try them for their wonderful flavour and scent. They remain hard until cooked

4 large quinces
1¼ cups/285ml/½ pt apple juice
1–3 tbsps mild clear honey

1¼ cups/285ml/½ pt double (heavy) cream

1   Preheat the oven to 150°C/300°F/Gas Mark 2.
2   Peel, core and slice the quinces, place in a casserole and pour in the apple juice. Cover with a well-fitting lid.
3   Bake in a slow oven or in the bottom oven of a solid fuel cooker until they are dark red and tender, usually 2–3 hours.
4   Remove from the oven and allow to cool.
5   Blend to a purée with the honey in a blender or food processor.
6   Whip the cream and stir lightly into the quince purée to give a marbled effect.
7   Spoon into serving glasses and chill before serving.

Winter Fruit Salad with Soft Cheese Serves 4

½ cup/75g/3 oz dried apricots
⅓ cup/50g/2 oz dried pears
1 cup/50g/2 oz dried apple rings
½ cup/50g/2 oz dried peaches

2 cups/425ml/¾ pt apple juice
2 clementines or satsumas
½ cup/100g/4 oz cream cheese
   or 8% fromage frais

1 Roughly chop the dried fruit and place in a large glass bowl.
2 Pour the apple juice over and leave to soak for 8–12 hours or overnight.
3 When needed, peel and divide the clementines or satsumas into segments, removing all pith. Add to the dried fruit.
4 Serve in individual bowls, topping each portion with a spoonful of cream cheese or fromage frais.

Suggestions for Packed Meals

Although not as mobile as the sandwich or cheese lunch, an alkaline meal, generally in the form of a soup or salad, can be quite easily transported in a thermos flask or plastic container.

There is a wide choice of soups and salads for alkaline meals in the recipe section; these, with the addition of the following ideas, will make a tasty and varied alkaline packed meal:

- Celery boats filled with a suitable dip or spread
- Avocado half with a compatible dressing and salad
- Muesli (granola) with fruit juice (see Alkaline Muesli Recipe page 31)
- Cream cheese and crudités

To follow, pack any compatible fruit such as apples, pears, oranges, fresh apricots or peaches, or a small container of raspberries or strawberries with Greek yoghurt. If still hungry, sun-dried raisins and sunflower seeds make a delicious filler.

Recipes for Protein Meals

V at the start of a recipe denotes vegetarian

This section contains recipes for protein meals and all the recipes are compatible with each other.

It is suggested that only one protein meal a day should be eaten. Dr Hay recommended that meat should be served not more than three times a week but, if combined with the right vegetables and fruits, more frequent servings will pose no problems for most people.

Mushrooms and nuts contain vegetable protein. Milk contains protein to the extent that it is not compatible with starches, except in limited amounts (for example the small quantity usually served with breakfast cereals). Because of the difference in the structure of milk protein it should *not* be served with a meal containing meat.

All green vegetables and salad greens combine well with protein meals; lists of these can be found in the Table of Compatible Foods on page 20. All sauces and dressings for vegetables and salads to be served with a protein meal should be selected only from this section.

Food and Drinks that Can be Combined for a Protein Meal

Proteins

Meat of all kinds, beef, lamb, pork, venison, chicken, turkey, game, eggs, cheese, fish, shellfish and soya products.

Note Some pork products are no longer recommended because of modern chemical 'curing' methods.

Acid Fruits

Apples, apricots (fresh and dried), cherries, pears, pineapples, grapes, lemons, oranges, peaches, strawberries, raspberries, mangoes, berries of all kinds, nectarines and tangerines (see comprehensive list in Table of Compatible Foods, page 20).

Vegetables

All green and root vegetables except potatoes and Jerusalem artichokes
All salad greens
Tomatoes: cooked and uncooked

Dairy Products

Milk and yoghurt, though protein, combine best with fruit and vegetables
and should not be served with a meat meal

Note Mushrooms, nuts, oils, raisins, unsalted butter, cream cheese,
cream, soured cream and egg yolks combine with all meals

Drinks

Tea, filter coffee (though not recommended), non-cereal coffee
substitutes (no sweetening permissible), herb teas
Soft drinks: tomato juice, grape juice, apple juice, unsweetened orange
juice, unsweetened lemon juice and water, unsweetened lime juice
and water, unsweetened grapefruit juice, raisin juice
Alcoholic drinks: all dry light red wines, all dry white wines, dry cider,
whisky, gin, rum, brandy, vodka
Spring water: combines equally well with all classes of food. Carbonated
waters also combine but are not recommended.

Apple and Apricot Muesli

(Granola) (V) Makes 450g/1 lb (US 4 cups)

1 cup/50g/2 oz dried apple, cut into small pieces

½ cup/75g/3 oz dried apricots, cut into small pieces

¾ cup/75g/3 oz flaked (slivered) almonds, finely chopped

¼ cup/25g/1 oz pumpkin seeds, finely chopped

⅓ cup/50g/2 oz sun-dried raisins

¼ cup/25g/1 oz sunflower seeds

½ cup/50g/2 oz sesame seeds

½ cup/50g/2 oz hazelnuts, roasted and finely chopped

1 Mix all together and store in an airtight container.

Serve with milk, diluted cream or fruit juice.

Egg Savoury (v) Serves 2

A rather luxurious version of 'scrambled eggs'! (v)

1 tsp barley or rice miso
2 tsps tahini
pinch paprika
4 large eggs, beaten

1 tbsp unsalted butter
½ cup/50g/2 oz Cheddar cheese, finely
   grated
freshly ground black pepper

1 Mix together the miso, tahini and paprika until smooth.
2 Add to the beaten eggs and combine thoroughly using a whisk or fork
   – the miso may not mix in completely at this stage, but will do so on
   cooking.
3 Melt the unsalted butter in a pan, add the egg mix and scramble over a
   low heat until the desired consistency is achieved.
4 Remove from the heat, stir in the grated cheese and season with
   pepper.

Serve on starch-free crackers (see page 142) or on slices of tomato or
cucumber. Alternatively grill (broil) or bake aubergine (eggplant) slices
until tender, pile the egg mixture on top and heat through. These eggs
make a tasty protein topping for vegetables, or serve cold and spread on
starch-free crackers.

This is also an ideal light lunch or evening meal or a quick main
course.

This recipe does not produce a large portion of scrambled eggs, but
the mixture is fairly rich: if a larger portion is desired an extra egg per
person can be added without lessening the flavour.

Note:
Barley or rice miso is a soybean paste made by fermenting soybeans with
barley or rice. Only a small amount is needed.

Pineapple and Kiwi Fruit Cream (v) Serves 2–3

2 cups/225g/8 oz pineapple, cleaned
   weight, cored and roughly chopped
1½ cups/225g/8 oz kiwi fruit, peeled and
   chopped

½ cup/50g/2 oz ground almonds
honey or maple syrup to taste (optional
   and only if used sparingly)

1 Place the pineapple in a food processor or blender and blend until
   smooth.
2 Add the kiwi fruit and blend again until completely broken down and
   the mixture is very smooth.
3 Stir in the ground almonds, sweeten to taste if desired, then chill
   before serving.

Also good served as a dessert topped with yoghurt, cream or ice-cream
and some extra chopped pineapple or kiwi fruit.

Additional Protein Breakfast Suggestions

- Grated cheese mixed with diced apple tossed in freshly squeezed lemon juice and served with starch-free crackers (page 142) (v)
- Carrot and/or celery stalks with a piece of fresh fruit(v)
- Starch-free crackers with sugar-free jam, marmalade, yeast extract, etc. (v)
- Eggs – boiled, scrambled, poached or fried, served with starch-free crackers, grilled (broiled) or fried tomatoes and fried mushrooms or onions (v)
- Fresh fruit, served alone or with milk, yoghurt, cream or diluted cream (v)
- Onion, tomato and mushrooms fried, then topped with cheese and placed under a grill (broiler) until the cheese is golden and bubbly (v)
- Prunes soaked in unsweetened orange juice (v)
- Fresh grapefruit, followed by scrambled egg with grilled (broiled) mushrooms (v)
- Fresh pears, followed by steamed plaice with grilled (broiled) tomatoes
- Grapefruit segments, followed by grilled (broiled) herring
- Sliced apple, followed by Finnan haddock and a poached egg

Chilled Courgette (Zucchini) Soup (v) Serves 4

Use only small, fresh courgettes (zucchini) for this early summer soup

1 lb/450g courgettes (zucchini), sliced
2½ cups/570ml/1 pt spring water
1 small onion, chopped
1 yellow pepper, skinned, deseeded
   and sliced

1¼ cups/285ml/½ pt Greek yoghurt
sea salt and freshly ground black pepper
chopped fresh mint to garnish

1   Put the courgettes (zucchini), water and onion into a pan and bring to
    the boil. Simmer gently until the courgettes (zucchini) are just tender,
    but still crunchy and light green.
2   Remove from the heat and cool.
3   Using a blender or food processor, blend the courgettes (zucchini)
    and their cooking water with the sliced pepper.
4   Stir in the yoghurt and adjust the seasoning.
5   Pour into individual bowls and chill.
6   Sprinkle with chopped mint to serve.

Chilled Cucumber Soup (v) Serves 3–4

1 large cucumber, peeled and chopped
1 clove garlic, crushed
⅔ cup/150ml/¼ pt plain yoghurt
1 tbsp finely chopped fresh mint or
    tarragon

sea salt and freshly ground black pepper
3–4 tbsps creamy milk

1 Place the cucumber, garlic and yoghurt into a blender or food
   processor and whizz to a purée.
2 Stir in the herb of your choice and season according to taste.
3 Thin to the right consistency with the milk and chill thoroughly before
   serving.

Courgette (Zucchini) and Carrot Soup (v) Serves 4

1 tbsp olive oil
1 onion, sliced
2 cloves garlic, chopped
1 lb/450g courgettes (zucchini), grated
(shredded)

2 large carrots, grated (shredded)
3¾ cups/850ml/1½ pts spring water
freshly ground black pepper
1 tbsp chopped fresh basil

1   Using a thick-based pan, heat the oil, add the onion and garlic and
    cook gently until softened but not brown.
2   Add the courgettes (zucchini) and carrots and turn them in the oil for
    2–3 minutes.
3   Add the water and season generously with the pepper. Bring to the
    boil, cover and simmer for 10–15 minutes.
4   Stir in the chopped basil, simmer for a further 5 minutes and serve.

For a smooth soup, blend in the blender or food processor.

Cauliflower and Parsnip Soup (v) Serves 4–6

An unusual and warming white soup for Winter

1 tbsp olive oil
1 medium onion, chopped
1 small cauliflower
2 medium parsnips
3¾ cups/850ml/1½ pts spring water

sea salt and freshly ground black pepper
freshly grated nutmeg or mace
2 tbsps single (light) cream
chopped fresh parsley to garnish

1   Heat the oil in a large pan. Add the onion and cook over a low heat
    until it is transparent.
2   Clean the cauliflower and parsnips and slice. Add the vegetables
    and water and bring gently to the boil. Cover and simmer until the
    vegetables are soft, about 20–30 minutes.
3   Remove from the heat, cool slightly and, using a blender or food
    processor, blend until smooth.
4   Pour back into the rinsed-out pan and add seasoning and a little
    grated nutmeg or mace to taste.
5   Stir in the cream and serve very hot, garnished with chopped parsley.

Freezing:
This soup can be frozen if the cream is omitted, then added when ready
for serving.

Creamy Celery and Walnut Soup (v) Serves 4–6

The beautiful, rich flavour of walnuts makes this a rather special soup

2 tbsps olive or sunflower oil

1½ cups/175g/6 oz onions, finely chopped

1 lb/450g celery, cut into strips then thinly sliced

1 vegetable stock (bouillon) cube

¼ cup/25g/1 oz ground almonds

1½ cups/175g/6 oz walnuts, finely ground

5 cups/1 L/2 pt boiling spring water

sea salt and freshly ground black pepper

1 Heat the oil in a thick-based pan and add the onion and celery. Cover and cook gently for 20 minutes, stirring occasionally.
2 Crumble in the stock (bouillon) cube, then stir in the ground almonds and walnuts.
3 Remove the pan from the heat and slowly stir in the water.
4 Return to the heat, bring to the boil and simmer for 10–15 minutes, until the celery is tender. Season to taste.

Serve the soup as prepared or place in a food processor or blender and blend until smooth, adding more stock or water if necessary. Accompany with starch-free crackers.

For a light lunch or evening meal serve as above, followed by a salad.

Freezing:
Can be frozen.

Onion Soup (v) Serves 6

Another variation on a traditional recipe, the addition of spices gives this soup a lovely warm, round flavour

3 tbsps/40g/1½ oz unsalted butter
2½ lb/1 kg onions, halved and thinly
   sliced in short lengths
1 tsp paprika
½ tsp garam masala

½ tsp ground cumin
2 vegetable stock (bouillon) cubes
5 cups/1 L/2 pts spring water
sea salt and freshly ground black pepper

1 Melt the unsalted butter in a large pan and sweat the onions, covered for 20 minutes, or until very soft.
2 Add the spices and crumble in the stock (bouillon) cubes.
3 Stir in the water and bring to the boil. Season, cover and simmer for 20 minutes and serve.

Freezing:
Can be frozen.

Tomato Cups (v) Serves 4

Use the large continental beefsteak tomatoes for this dish. If you grow your own, the outdoor variety 'Marmande' has a good flavour and stores well. The Italian cream cheese Mascarpone is excellent for this, but any real cream cheese will do well; however, not cottage cheese

2 beefsteak tomatoes
½ cup/100g/4 oz cream cheese
freshly ground black pepper
1 cup/100g/4 oz cucumber, peeled
   and diced

2 finely chopped fresh chives
1 tbsp finely chopped fresh basil
2 tbsps fromage frais
frisée or watercress

1   Cut the tomatoes in halves and scoop out the seeds. Discard the seeds and drain the tomato cups upside down on absorbent paper.
2   Mix the cream cheese, black pepper, cucumber, chives and basil together. If the mixture is too stiff, thin it to a smoother consistency with the fromage frais.
3   Fill the tomato cups with the mixture and serve on a bed of frisée or watercress.

Cream Cheese Apple Rings (v) Serves 4

4 dessert apples (such as Russets)
juice of ½ lemon
½ cup/100g/4 oz cream cheese

⅓ cup/50g/2 oz sun-dried raisins
½ cup/50g/2 oz walnuts
chopped lettuce

1 Peel the apples thinly, remove the core and cut across to make rings.
2 Brush the apple rings with a little lemon juice and arrange on a bed of lettuce or individual serving plates.
3 Mix the cream cheese with the raisins and chopped nuts and place a small heap on each apple ring.
4 Serve immediately.

Marinated Courgettes (Zucchini) (v) Serves 4

Use very small, young courgettes (zucchini) for this refreshing summer first course

½ cup/125ml/4 fl oz olive oil
2 tsps freshly squeezed lime juice
1 clove garlic, crushed
1 tbsp chopped fresh parsley
1 tbsp chopped fresh basil

sea salt and freshly ground black pepper
1½ lb/675g small courgettes (zucchini)
2 firm tomatoes, skinned, deseeded and
  chopped

1   Put the oil, lime juice, garlic, herbs, and seasoning into a screw-topped jar and shake well.
2   Slice the courgettes (zucchini) diagonally into 4–5 cm/1½–2-in lengths.
3   Place in a steamer and steam for 4–5 minutes. They should remain very firm and bright green.
4   Drain the courgettes (zucchini) and while still hot divide between individual dishes. Pour the dressing over.
5   Leave to cool then top each dish with a little chopped tomato.

Carrot, Walnut and Sage Pâté (v) Serves 4

A moist pâté with a rich earthy flavour of walnuts

1 tbsp olive or sunflower oil
1 cup/100g/4 oz onions, very finely
    chopped
2 cups/225g/8 oz carrots, finely diced
1 tsp low-sea salt yeast extract

1½ tbsps finely chopped fresh sage
2 tsps tamari
sea salt and freshly ground black pepper
1 cup/100g/4 oz ground walnuts

1   Heat the oil and fry the onion until soft.
2   Add the carrot, cover and cook for 10–15 minutes or until tender,
    stirring occasionally.
3   Mix in the yeast extract, sage and tamari and cook for a further
    2 minutes. Season.
4   Remove the pan from the heat and stir in the walnuts.
5   Leave to cool slightly then place the mixture in a food processor or
    blender and blend until smooth.
6   Cool completely and chill before serving.

Garnish the pâté with sage leaves, chopped sage, walnut halves and
carrot circles, and serve with crudités or starch-free crackers (see page
142).

Scoop into balls using an ice-cream scoop, or present in a bowl or
individual ramekins, or turn out on to a serving plate; to do this line a
bowl with cling film (Saran wrap), fill with the pâté, chill for 3–4 hours
then invert on to the serving plate and peel away the cling film (Saran
wrap) to produce a moulded shape.

The pâté will keep for 4–5 days in the refrigerator.

Freezing:
Can be frozen.

Spicy Tahini and Tamari Dip (v) Serves 4

A lovely, savoury dip

¾ cup/175g/6 oz soft silken tofu
1½ tbsps light tahini
2 tsps tamari

½ tsp paprika
freshly ground black pepper

1 Place all the ingredients in a food processor or blender and blend until smooth.

Serve with crudités or starch-free crackers (see page 142).
  This dip is also delicious as a protein-rich vegetable topping.

Aubergine (Eggplant) Pâté (v) Serves 4–6

Basil and rosemary complement the earthy flavour of aubergine (eggplant) beautifully in this dish

¼ cup/3 tbsps olive oil

2 cups/225g/8 oz onions, very finely chopped

1 lb/450g aubergine (eggplant), cut into small cubes

1½ tbsps finely chopped fresh basil or 3 tsps dried basil

1 tbsp finely chopped fresh rosemary or 1½ tsps dried rosemary

½ vegetable stock (bouillon) cube

¼ cup/3 tbsps freshly squeezed lemon juice

1 tbsp tomato purée

sea salt and freshly ground black pepper

1　Heat the oil in a large pan and add the onion and aubergine (eggplant). Cover and cook for 15–20 minutes over a low heat until soft.

2　Mix in the remaining ingredients, combine thoroughly and cook for a further 5 minutes.

3　Place the mixture in a food processor or blender and blend until smooth.

4　Leave to cool, then serve as a pâté or dip with crudités or starch-free crackers (see page 142).

Also excellent as a vegetable topping.

Freezing:
Can be frozen.

Leeks à l'Orange
with a Thyme Vinaigrette (v) Serves 4

A delectable way to serve leeks – excellent for a dinner party first course

8 thin leeks, weighing approximately
675g/1½ lb (cleaned weight) in total
⅔ cup/150ml/¼ pt unsweetened orange
juice
3 tbsps/40g/1½ oz unsalted butter, cut
into small pieces

4 bay leaves
freshly ground black pepper
2 oranges, segmented, to garnish

Thyme Vinaigrette
½ cup/100ml/4 fl oz olive oil
2 tbsps cider vinegar

1 tsp coarse grain mustard
1 tsp dried thyme
freshly ground black pepper

1   Preheat the oven to 190°C/375°F/Gas Mark 5.
2   Cut each leek in half and place in the base of an ovenproof dish. Pour
    the orange juice over the leeks.
3   Top with the unsalted butter and bay leaves (split to release their
    flavour) and season with pepper.
4   Cover the dish with foil and bake in the oven for 1 hour or until tender.
5   Prepare the vinaigrette by mixing together all the ingredients.
6   Remove the bay leaves, arrange the cooked leeks on four heated
    plates, pour the vinaigrette on top and garnish with orange segments.

This dish is delicious served as a first course, but can equally be served as
a vegetable if returned to the oven after being tossed in the vinaigrette to
heat through thoroughly. (If serving as a vegetable it is best to cut the
leeks into thick rounds instead of just in half.)

Cucumber and Tarragon Salad (v) Serves 4

A very light summer first course or a good accompaniment to a dish of cold salmon or trout

2 large cucumbers, peeled and thinly sliced
⅔ cup/150ml/¼ pt soured cream

sea salt and freshly ground black pepper
1 tbsp chopped fresh tarragon

1   Put the cucumber into a serving bowl.
2   Season the soured cream with a little sea salt and pepper.
3   Mix in the chopped tarragon and pour this mixture over the cucumber.
4   If possible, chill for an hour before serving.

Carrot, Apple and Raisin Salad (v) Serves 4–6

This must be one of the quickest and cheapest salads to make –
and children simply love it!

1 lb/450g carrots, coarsely grated (shredded)	2–3 tbsps sun-dried raisins
2 crisp dessert apples (Russets are good)	⅔ cup/150ml/¼ pt soured cream
	2 tsps chopped fresh mint

1   Place the carrots in a serving bowl.
2   Peel and finely dice the apples and mix with the carrots.
3   Add the raisins, stir in the soured cream and mint, and leave for a few
    minutes for the flavours to blend.

Chicory (Endive) and Orange Salad (v) Serves 4–6

1 or 2 heads of chicory
2 ripe oranges, preferably seedless
French Dressing (page 93)

1 Wash and trim the chicory (endive).
2 Separate the leaves and cut in half across if they are very long.
3 Peel the oranges and cut into thin slices.
4 Arrange the chicory (endive) leaves and orange slices in a dish; pour over just enough dressing to coat the ingredients thoroughly.

This salad can be made an hour or so before it is needed if kept in a cool place.

Fennel and Radish Salad (v) Serves 4

This crisp salad makes an unusual first course or a good accompaniment to a main course

2 bulbs fennel, peeled
2 bunches radishes
¼ cup/3 tbsps olive oil

2 tbsps freshly squeezed lemon juice
sea salt and freshly ground black pepper

1 Put the fennel into iced water for 30 minutes to keep it crisp.
2 Wash and trim the radishes and slice thinly (the round globe radishes are best for this).
3 Slice the fennel thinly and arrange with the radishes on a flat serving dish.
4 Mix the oil and lemon juice with salt and pepper to taste and spoon over the salad.

Spiced Red Cabbage and Walnut Salad (v) Serves 4–6

½ small red cabbage, finely grated
(shredded)
2 stalks celery, chopped
¼ cup/25g/1 oz walnuts, broken

¼ tsp freshly grated nutmeg
Yoghurt Dressing (page 92)
sea salt and freshly ground black pepper

1 Mix the first four ingredients together and toss in sufficient yoghurt dressing to coat thoroughly.
2 Add salt and pepper to taste if necessary.

Leeks and Fennel tossed in a Walnut and Tarragon Dressing (v) Serves 4

Tarragon and walnuts beautifully complement the delicate flavour of leeks and fennel

2 tbsps olive or sunflower oil
2½ cups/275g/10 oz leeks, cleaned
   weight, thinly sliced
1 cup/100g/4 oz fennel, thinly sliced
½ cup/50g/2 oz walnuts, finely chopped

sea salt and freshly ground black pepper
Walnut and Tarragon Dressing (page 90)
walnut halves and fresh tarragon to
   garnish

1 Heat the oil in a thick-based pan and add the leeks and fennel. Cover and cook for 5–10 minutes until tender, stirring occasionally.
2 Add the chopped walnuts and season to taste.
3 Pour the dressing over the hot vegetables and turn into a serving dish.
4 Leave to cool then chill for 3–4 hours to allow the flavours to blend.
5 Remove from the refrigerator 30 minutes before serving and garnish with walnut halves and fresh tarragon if available.

Serve as a first course on a bed of lettuce in individual glass dishes, or on small plates with a salad garnish. Accompany with starch-free crackers. It can also be served as a vegetable accompaniment to main course dishes, and with salad for a light lunch or evening meal.

Freezing:
Freeze the cooked leek and fennel mixture only; heat through once thawed, add the chopped walnuts and dressing and proceed as described above.

Walnut and Tarragon Dressing (v) Serves 4

A very flavoursome dressing

⅓ cup/4 tbsps walnut oil

2 tsps finely chopped fresh tarragon
or 1 tsp dried tarragon

2 tbsps cider or rice vinegar

sea salt and freshly ground black pepper

1 Mix all the ingredients together then refrigerate for 1 hour to let the flavours blend.

Especially good over green salads and as a dressing on hard-boiled eggs.

Thyme Vinaigrette (v) Serves 4

A lovely, sharp vinaigrette – very much a favourite of ours

½ cup/125ml/4 fl oz olive oil
2 tbsps cider vinegar
1 tsp coarse grain mustard

1 tsp dried thyme
freshly ground black pepper

1 Shake the ingredients together in a screw-topped jar, then set aside for
   1 hour to let the flavours blend.

Yoghurt Dressing (v) Makes about 150ml/¼ pt (US ⅔ cup)

This is a quickly made dressing – delicious on grated (shredded) root vegetable salads

2 tsps freshly squeezed lemon juice
sea salt and freshly ground black pepper
⅔ cup/150ml/¼ pt plain yoghurt

mixed fresh herbs of choice, finely
chopped

1   Mix the lemon juice with the salt and pepper. Stir in the yoghurt and chopped herbs and pour this mixture over the prepared salad.

This dressing can be varied by the use of different herbs: chopped winter savory enhances a salad of green beans; tarragon, thyme or oregano lift most root vegetable salads; and a few chopped chives or half a finely chopped shallot give an extra bite to the flavour.

French Dressing (v)

½ tsp sea salt
1 clove garlic, crushed (optional)
1 tsp Dijon mustard
2 tbsps freshly squeezed lemon juice or
    cider vinegar

freshly ground black pepper
½ cup/6 tbsps extra virgin olive oil or
    cold-pressed sunflower seed oil

1   Put all the ingredients into a screw-topped jar and shake vigorously.

This amount should be enough to dress two salads or more and can be stored in the refrigerator for a few days.

Variation:
If you prefer a sweeter dressing, a teaspoon of clear honey can be added to the basic recipe. Chopped chives or a little chopped shallot may be substituted for the garlic.

Fast Mayonnaise (v) Makes about 285ml/¹/₂ pt (US 1¹/₄ cups)

2 egg yolks at room temperature
1 tsp dry mustard
pinch sea salt
freshly ground black pepper

1 tbsp freshly squeezed lemon juice
1¹/₄ cups/285ml/¹/₂ pt extra virgin olive oil
1 tbsp boiling spring water

1   Put the egg yolks, mustard and seasoning into a blender.
2   Add the lemon juice and blend the ingredients together at the lowest
    speed.
3   Remove the centre cap of the blender goblet and, with the motor
    running at lowest speed, pour the oil onto the egg mixture *very slowly*
    – almost drop by drop.
4   Continue to add the oil very slowly until the mixture begins to thicken.
5   Add the rest of the oil in a steady stream and lastly add the boiling
    water. Switch off the blender.

This mayonnaise will keep well in the refrigerator if covered.

Variation:
For an interesting variation, the addition of a couple of tablespoons of
chopped green herbs such as parsley, sorrel, chives or young spinach
leaves, after the mayonnaise has thickened, will transform it into a *sauce
verte;* this can be used as a salad dressing or as an accompaniment to
cold trout, salmon or chicken.

Avocado and Grapefruit Salad (v) Serves 4

1 ripe avocado   ½ cup/100g/4 oz cream cheese
1 large or 2 small grapefruit   crisp lettuce leaves
2–3 tbsps French Dressing (page 93)   paprika

1   Peel and slice the avocado, removing the stone, and mix with the
    French dressing.
2   Peel the grapefruit, discarding all the pith, and separate into segments;
    remove the skin and pips.
3   Add the grapefruit segments to the avocado and toss carefully
    together.
4   Shape the cream cheese into four small balls.
5   Arrange crisp lettuce leaves on individual plates and divide the salad
    between them.
6   Place a cream cheese ball in the centre of each salad and sprinkle with
    paprika.

Chicken Salad with Herb Dressing Serves 2

This is a quick and delicious way of serving leftover chicken

2 cups/225g/8 oz cold cooked chicken,
  cut into bite-sized pieces
salad leaves: 2 varieties of lettuce plus
  radicchio, Chinese leaf, rocket and a
  few fresh sorrel leaves
⅔ cup/150ml/¼ pt Mayonnaise (page 94)

2 tsps Dijon mustard
2 tbsps plain yoghurt
2 tbsps mixed chopped fresh herbs:
  chives, tarragon, parsley, lovage
sea salt and freshly ground black pepper

1 Pile the chicken pieces in the centre of a large serving bowl.
2 Wash and dry the salad leaves and arrange round the chicken.
3 Mix the mayonnaise, mustard and yoghurt together and stir in the
   chopped herbs.
4 Test for seasoning and add a little sea salt and pepper if necessary.
5 Pour the dressing over the chicken and serve.

A side salad of courgettes (zucchini) and tomatoes goes well with this
dish.

Avocados
and Walnuts (v) Serves 4 as a first course or 2 as a light meal

10 fresh walnuts

1 clove garlic, finely chopped

2 tbsps walnut oil

2 tsps cider vinegar

freshly ground black pepper

2 ripe avocados

crisp lettuce leaves

1   Shell the walnuts and reserve 4 walnut halves.

2   Using a food processor (or pestle and mortar) reduce the remaining nuts to a paste. Add the garlic, oil, vinegar and pepper and mix well.

3   Halve and stone the avocados. Fill the centres of the avocados with the mixture and top with the reserved walnut halves.

4   Serve at once on a bed of crisp lettuce leaves.

Recipes for Protein Meals / LIGHT MEAL SALADS

Egg and Tomato Salad (v) Serves 4

6 eggs, hard-boiled and chopped
1 lb/450g cherry tomatoes, quartered
1 shallot or ½ Spanish onion, thinly sliced
¼ cup/3 tbsps extra virgin olive oil

1 tbsp cider vinegar
sea salt and freshly ground black pepper
finely chopped fresh tarragon or basil

1 Place the eggs and tomatoes in a serving bowl and carefully mix in the onion.
2 Mix together the olive oil, vinegar, seasoning and herbs, and combine well.
3 Pour the dressing over the salad and leave to stand for a few minutes before serving.

Emergency Tuna Salad
Serves 4 as a first course or 2 as a light meal

This quickly assembled and delicious salad is a useful emergency standby from the store cupboard

2 crisp, dessert apples, peeled and
   chopped
4 stalks celery, chopped
1 cup/200g/7 oz canned tuna in brine,
   drained and flaked

½ cup/50g/2 oz walnut halves
⅔ cup/150ml/¼ pt Mayonnaise (page 94)
lettuce to serve

1   Mix all the ingredients together, reserving a few walnut halves for
    garnish.
2   Serve on a bed of lettuce on individual serving plates and garnish with
    the reserved walnut halves.

Fish

If you are fortunate enough to have a local market or fish stall please *use it*. Fresh fish is one of the most varied, flavoursome and healthy protein foods you can buy. It needs very little cooking: plain grilling, steaming or oven-baking in foil are usually all it requires. In fact it meets all the needs of the fast Hay cook.

Make a firm friend of your fishmonger, who, if consulted, will advise you, prepare your chosen fish and, if you order in advance, bring you the more unusual catches to try. It would have been impossible to prepare the recipes included without the help and encouragement of Mr Bunning in Norfolk and his colleagues who cheerfully produced and, if necessary, filleted some of the more unusual requests. Our thanks to them for their interest and encouragement.

If you are new to fish cookery or unsure about what to look for, Jean recommends that you use *The Fish Course* by Susan Hicks, who not only explains what to buy and how to prepare it, but offers a wealth of fish recipes easily adaptable for Hay followers.

Trout Fillets poached in Cider Serves 4

This simple way of cooking trout fillets is a delicious alternative to the ubiquitous trout with almonds, and is popular with the members of the family who don't like having to deal with bones

4 medium fillets of trout, 175g/6 oz each in weight
freshly ground black pepper
⅓ cup/4 tbsps dry cider

4 sprigs fresh tarragon
½ cup/6 tbsps 8% fromage frais
watercress and lemon wedges to garnish

1 Preheat the oven to 180°C/350°F/Gas Mark 4.
2 Rinse the trout fillets and pat dry with absorbent paper.
3 Season lightly on both sides with the black pepper and lay them in a buttered flameproof dish.
4 Pour the cider over the fillets and place a sprig of tarragon on each one.
5 Cover the dish loosely with a sheet of foil and place in the preheated oven. After 10 minutes remove foil and cook for a further 10 minutes.
6 Remove from the oven and transfer the fillets to a warmed serving dish.
7 Return the cooking dish to a low heat and add the fromage frais. Stir gently to mix the juices and to warm through, adjust seasoning and pour this liquid over the fillets. Serve garnished with watercress and lemon wedges.

Halibut Salad Serves 4–6

This green and white salad makes an attractive first course or a light main course for a summer meal. It would also make a very pretty addition to a cold buffet

1½ lb/675g halibut, about 2.5cm/
  1 in thick
½ cup/4 tbsps extra virgin olive oil
2 tbsps freshly squeezed lemon juice
freshly ground black pepper

sea salt (optional)
⅓ cup/4 tbsps chopped fresh mixed
  herbs: tarragon, dill, chives, coriander
  (cilantro) leaves or parsley

1 Preheat the oven to 180°C/350°F/Gas Mark 4.
2 Rinse the fish and pat dry with absorbent paper. Brush a large piece of foil with a little of the olive oil and place the fish in the middle.
3 Sprinkle the fish with a little of the lemon juice and some black pepper.
4 Make a loose parcel of the foil and place it on a rack in a roasting pan. Bake for 30 minutes. Remove from the oven and allow to cool before unwrapping the foil.
5 Flake the fish, discarding the skin and bones, and put into a serving bowl.
6 Mix in the oil and lemon juice very lightly so that the fish pieces do not break up too much.
7 Test for seasoning and adjust if necessary. Stir in the chopped herbs and serve.

Doris Grant's Creamed Smoked Haddock Serves 4

Smoked haddock is delicious prepared in this simple way

4 small or 2 large smoked haddock fillets
freshly ground black pepper
1¼ cups/285ml/½ pt milk

⅔ cup/150ml/¼ pt single (light) cream
sea salt (optional)
chopped fresh parsley to garnish

1　Preheat the oven to 180°C/350°F/Gas Mark 4.
2　Trim and rinse the haddock fillets and pat dry with absorbent paper.
3　Place the fillets in an ovenproof dish and season lightly with the black pepper.
4　Pour the milk over the fish and poach gently in the oven for about 15 minutes, or until the fish flakes easily.
5　Remove the fish from the oven and flake, using a fork. Discard the skin and any remaining liquids.
6　Transfer to a warmed buttered ovenproof dish, stir in the cream and adjust seasoning if necessary.
7　Return to the oven for a few minutes to heat through. Serve garnished with parsley.

Make sure the haddock has been oak smoked, not dyed. Very bright yellow haddock has been cured chemically and should not be used. Lightly steamed purple sprouting broccoli (when in season) dusted with a little grated nutmeg and served with a knob of unsalted butter makes a delicious accompaniment to this dish.

Lemon Sole with Dill Serves 4

This quickly prepared fish dish can be adjusted for any number of people. Allow one sole per person and adjust the other ingredients accordingly; the quantities are not critical

4 lemon soles, skinned and filleted
a little olive oil
¼ cup/50g/2 oz unsalted (sweet) butter

juice of 1 lime
1 tbsp chopped fresh dill

1 Preheat the oven to 180°C/350°F/Gas Mark 4.
2 Rinse the sole fillets and pat dry with absorbent paper.
3 Choose an ovenproof dish in which the fish will fit snugly, brush the dish with oil and arrange the fillets in it.
4 Melt the unsalted butter and stir in with the lime juice. Brush this mixture over the fish and sprinkle with the chopped dill.
5 Bake in the oven for approximately 20 minutes, until just cooked.

Serve with a dish of tiny broad (fava) beans dressed with a little melted unsalted butter, and Creamed Chard.

Sea Bass with Tarragon Serves 2

Most recipes for sea bass are rather daunting as it is a large, bony fish, usually prepared with a stuffing and cooked whole. However, if you see one weighing about 900g/2 lb or just under, ask your fishmonger to fillet it for you and try it this way. It has a superb texture and flavour

2 fillets of sea bass	2 tbsps chopped fresh tarragon
a little olive oil	and chervil
1 shallot or ½ small onion, finely chopped	½ cup/4 tbsps dry white wine

1 Preheat the oven to 190°C/375°F/Gas Mark 5.
2 Rinse and trim the fillets and pat dry with absorbent paper.
3 Oil a shallow ovenproof dish and place the fillets in it.
4 Spread a layer of chopped shallot or onion over both fillets, then a layer of chopped tarragon and chervil.
5 Pour the wine over the fish and cover loosely with foil.
6 Bake for approximately 20 minutes, removing the foil halfway through.

Serve with a selection of fresh steamed vegetables and a green salad.

Note:
Parsley can be used instead of chervil if unobtainable, but it is not so delicate in flavour.

Red Mullet au Beurre Blanc Serves 4

It was several weeks before Mr Bunning was able to produce some red mullet, but it was well worth waiting for. When you buy mullet, make sure that the livers are still intact – they are considered a great delicacy

4 red mullet, scaled and cleaned	⅔ cup/150ml/¼ pt dry white wine
sea salt and freshly ground black pepper	¼ cup/3 tbsps double (heavy) cream
a little olive oil	¼ cup/50g/2 oz unsalted (sweet) butter
4 shallots, thinly sliced	1 tbsp freshly squeezed lemon juice

1   Check that the mullet livers are in place and season the fish inside. Arrange on an oiled grill (broiler) rack, brush the fish with oil and season the outside.
2   Heat the grill (broiler).
3   In a small pan reduce the shallots and white wine over a moderate heat until the shallots are soft and there is no liquid left. Remove from the heat.
4   Grill (broil) the mullet under a moderate to high heat for about 5 minutes on each side. Remove to a warmed serving dish and carefully take out the livers.
5   Chop the livers and reserve.
6   Add the cream to the shallots and bring nearly to the boil. Add the unsalted butter, piece by piece, stirring all the time.
7   Season the mixture, stir in the lemon juice and chopped livers, pour over the fish and serve.

Poached Brill with a Green Sauce Serves 2

Brill is easy and quick to cook, with a slightly softer texture than the more expensive turbot

2 fillets of brill, trimmed
a little olive oil
freshly ground black pepper
juice of ½ lemon
1 shallot or 2 spring onions (scallions),
    finely chopped

1 tsp grated fresh root ginger
⅓ cup/4 tbsps dry cider
parsley to garnish

Green Sauce
1 tbsp chopped fresh sorrel
1 tbsp chopped fresh coriander (cilantro)
    leaves

juices of ½ lemon
½ cup/4 tbsps fromage frais
sea salt and freshly ground black pepper

1   Preheat the oven to 190°C/375°F/Gas Mark 5.
2   Rinse the fillets and pat dry with absorbent paper.
3   Oil a shallow flameproof dish and arrange the fillets in it. Sprinkle
    them with pepper and the lemon juice.
4   Top the fish with the shallot or spring onion (scallion), the ginger and
    the cider.
5   Cover the dish loosely with foil and bake in the oven for about
    20 minutes, removing the foil for the last 5 minutes.
6   Remove the fish from the oven, transfer to warmed plates and keep
    warm.
7   Transfer the juices that remain to a flameproof baking dish and stir in
    the chopped sorrel and coriander (cilantro), lemon juice and fromage
    frais.
8   Stir together and heat through; test for seasoning and adjust if
    necessary.
9   Pour half the sauce over each fillet, garnish with parsley and serve.

Grilled Salmon Steaks with Dill Serves 4

Although salmon is no longer the luxury it used to be, it is still delicious, and so easy to prepare

4 salmon steaks, 2.5cm/1 in thick
a little olive oil
1 tbsp unsalted butter

1 tbsp chopped fresh dill
1 tbsp chopped fresh parsley
1 tbsp freshly squeezed lemon juice

1 Preheat the grill (broiler) until really hot
2 Brush the salmon steaks with olive oil and grill (broil) for 5 minutes on each side.
3 Combine the unsalted butter, dill, parsley and lemon juice together, mixing well.
4 Place a quarter of the mixture on each hot salmon steak and serve at once.

A cucumber salad and a dish of garden peas would make perfect partners.

Easy Tarragon Chicken Serves 4

1 chicken, not more than 1.75kg/4 lb
   in weight
2 tbsps/25g/1 oz unsalted (sweet) butter
1 tbsp chopped fresh tarragon

1 clove garlic, chopped
sea salt and freshly ground black pepper
a little olive oil

1 Preheat the oven to 200°C/400°F/Gas Mark 6.
2 Clean and trim the chicken.
3 Combine together the unsalted butter, tarragon, garlic and seasoning.
4 Place this inside the chicken and secure each end with a small skewer.
5 Brush the skin of the chicken with olive oil, making sure it is evenly coated.
6 Lay the bird upside down on a grid in a roasting pan and roast for 1¼–1½ hours, turning it over and basting well at half time.

Tiny French (snap) beans and spring carrots, lightly steamed and tossed in a little unsalted butter, plus a mixed green salad, are all that is needed to accompany this succulent chicken dish.

Cream of Chicken Serves 2

2 cups/225g/8 oz cooked chicken, diced
2 cups/225g/8 oz petits pois, steamed
1 tbsp chopped fresh tarragon

1¼ cups/285ml/½ pt single (light) cream
sea salt and freshly ground black pepper
chopped fresh parsley to garnish

1 Preheat the oven to 180°C/350°F/Gas Mark 4.
2 Using a small casserole, arrange the chicken and petits pois in alternate layers, scattering each chicken layer with tarragon as you go.
3 Season the cream with sea salt and pepper and pour this over the chicken.
4 Bake for 20–25 minutes, until completely heated through.
5 Remove from the oven, garnish with chopped parsley and serve.

This quick and soothing supper dish is a good way of using up cold chicken; the quantities can be varied according to availability.

A mixed green salad goes well with this dish.

Chicken Breasts in Creamy Herb Sauce Serves 4

The use of fresh herbs lifts this dish out of the ordinary. You can vary the herbs according to season; tarragon always goes well with chicken but the use of thyme and marjoram or oregano makes an interesting change

2 tbsps olive oil
1 shallot, chopped
4 chicken breasts, skinned
2 tbsps chopped fresh mixed herbs
    (thyme and marjoram, or whatever is
    available)

½ cup/6 tbsps dry cider
⅔ cup/140ml/¼ pt soured cream
sea salt and freshly ground black pepper

1   Preheat the oven to 200°C/400°F/Gas Mark 6.
2   Using a shallow flameproof dish, heat the olive oil and sauté the chopped shallot gently until it starts to soften.
3   Add the chicken breasts and fry lightly on both sides to colour them.
4   Sprinkle the chopped herbs and pour the cider over the chicken breasts.
5   Cover loosely with foil and bake in the oven for about 25–30 minutes, until the chicken feels tender and is cooked through.
6   Remove from the oven and put the chicken breasts on to a warmed serving dish or individual plates.
7   Using the juices that remain in the dish, mix in the soured cream and heat through, stirring gently. Test for seasoning and adjust if necessary.
8   Pour the sauce over the chicken and serve.

Casserole of Pheasant in Red Wine Serves 4–6

Pheasant roasted in the usual way can be very dry. This casserole takes minimal preparation and the result is moist and delicious

2 tbsps olive oil
2 shallots or 1 onion, chopped
2 young pheasants
sea salt and freshly ground black pepper
1 bay leaf

1 tsp chopped fresh thyme or ½ tsp dried thyme
⅔ cup/150ml/¼ pt red wine
spring water
1 lb/450g button mushrooms, halved

1 Preheat the oven to 180°C/350°F/Gas Mark 4.
2 Gently heat the olive oil in a flameproof casserole just large enough to hold the birds, add the shallots or onion and turn in the oil until transparent.
3 Wash and trim the pheasants. Season well with sea salt and pepper and place breast side down in the casserole.
4 Add the bay leaf and thyme and pour the wine over the birds. Add enough water just to cover them.
5 Cover the casserole with a well-fitting lid and cook in the preheated oven for 1½ hours.
6 Halfway through the cooking time, turn the birds breast side uppermost and add the mushrooms.
7 Remove from the oven and transfer pheasants and mushrooms to a heated serving dish, taking out the bay leaf.
8 Check the casserole juices for seasoning and adjust if necessary. Strain and serve separately.

Coriander Lamb Serves 4–6

This makes a delicious Sunday lunch in the summer when the first garden peas are ready

1 leg of spring lamb
2 cloves garlic, finely chopped
1 tbsp crushed coriander seeds

sea salt and freshly ground black pepper
a little extra virgin olive oil

1 Preheat the oven to 190°C/375°F/Gas Mark 5.
2 Cut a few small incisions in the meat and insert a mixture of the garlic and coriander seeds into each one.
3 Dust the joint lightly with a little salt and black pepper. Brush over with olive oil.
4 Place the meat on a rack in a roasting pan and roast for 20–25 minutes per pound, basting from time to time and turning the joint over halfway through.
5 Carve thick slices and serve with fresh garden peas and baby carrots.

A mixed green salad goes well after the main dish, with fresh fruit in season to follow.

Lamb Cutlets (Rib Lamb Chops)
with Mint Butter Serves 4

Ask your butcher for lamb cutlets from the best end of neck and to trim
them of surplus fat

¼ cup/50g/2 oz unsalted (sweet) butter
1 heaped tbsp chopped fresh mint
sea salt and freshly ground black pepper

2 tsps freshly squeezed lemon juice
8 trimmed lamb cutlets (rib lamb chops)

1 Using a pestle and mortar, pound the unsalted butter and mint to a
   smooth paste.
2 Season with a pinch of sea salt, some ground black pepper and the
   lemon juice.
3 Score the cutlets (chops) lightly on both sides and spread with the
   unsalted butter.
4 If possible, leave in a cool place for 1 hour.
5 Heat the grill (broiler) and cook the cutlets (chops) on each side –
   close to the grill (broiler) to start with, then further from the heat to
   finish, about 10 minutes in all.

Serve with a tomato salad and fresh garden peas.

Venison with Soured Cream Serves 6–8

This makes a splendid and unusual dinner party dish for a winter's evening. Venison is naturally low in fat and should be cooked fairly fast

2½ lb/1¼ kg/2½ lb venison (any cut), cut into cubes about 3cm/1¼ in thick
⅓ cup/4 tbsps extra virgin olive oil
2 large onions, sliced
freshly ground black pepper
2½ cups/570ml/1 pt vegetable stock (broth)

⅔ cup/150ml/¼ pt dry white wine or dry cider
1 lb/450g small mushrooms, wiped or peeled and left whole
1¼ cups/285ml/½ pt soured cream
sea salt to taste

1 Preheat the oven to 180°C/350°F/Gas Mark 4.
2 Heat the oil in a flameproof casserole and brown the pieces of venison, a few at a time. Remove and keep warm.
3 Add the onions to the casserole and cook for about 5 minutes, stirring until softened.
4 Add the pepper, stock and white wine or cider and bring slowly to the boil, stirring occasionally.
5 Return the meat to the casserole, cover with a tightly fitting lid and cook in the preheated oven for 50 minutes.
6 Remove from the oven and add the mushrooms. Simmer over a low heat for a further 10 minutes, uncovered.
7 Stir in the soured cream, adjust seasoning and serve.

A green salad, Crispy Oven Parsnips (page 133) and a Celeriac Purée (page 132) are good with this dish.

Freezing:
This dish will freeze provided you do not add the soured cream until after defrosting and reheating.

Beef Stroganoff with Tarragon Serves 4

1 tbsp olive oil
2 tbsps/25g/1 oz unsalted (sweet) butter
4 thin slices lean fillet of beef (sirloin), cut
   into 5-mm/¼-in strips
½ yellow pepper, deseeded and thinly
   sliced
4 cups/225g/8 oz button mushrooms,
   quartered

6 spring onions (scallions) or 2 shallots,
   thinly sliced
1 tbsp chopped fresh tarragon
⅔ cup/150ml/¼ pt soured cream
sea salt and freshly ground black pepper

1   Use a thick-based frying pan, heat the olive oil and add the unsalted butter.
2   When the unsalted butter is bubbling, add the beef and cook over a high heat for 2–3 minutes, turning the pieces to brown both sides.
3   Add the sliced peppers, mushrooms, spring onions (scallions) or shallots and the tarragon. Cook together for a further 3–4 minutes.
4   Finally, stir in the soured cream and seasoning, bring back nearly to boiling point and serve.

Tarragon Baked Eggs (v)

Serves 4 as a first course or 2 as a light meal

This quickly prepared variation on an old favourite makes a good first course or a light supper dish

⅓ cup/4 tbsps double (heavy) cream
sea salt and freshly ground black pepper
2 tbsps Parmesan cheese, freshly grated

1–2 tsps chopped fresh tarragon
4 large fresh eggs

1 Preheat the oven to 190°C/375°F/Gas Mark 5.
2 Heat the cream gently in a small saucepan, just enough to warm through.
3 Season with a pinch of sea salt and some pepper and add the grated cheese.
4 Divide the mixture between four buttered ramekins.
5 Scatter chopped tarragon over each ramekin and break an egg carefully into each one.
6 Place the ramekins in a shallow ovenproof dish and pour in enough hot water to come two-thirds of the way up the sides. Bake in the preheated oven for 7–10 minutes, until the eggs are just set.

Serve on its own as a first course or with a dish of grilled (broiled) mushrooms for a main course.

Scrambled Eggs with Parmesan (v) Serves 2

Another delicious variation on an old favourite

4 very fresh eggs
sea salt and freshly ground black pepper
2 tbsps/30g/1 oz unsalted (sweet) butter

1 tbsp double (heavy) cream
¼ cup/30g/1 oz Parmesan cheese, freshly
  grated

1 Break the eggs into a bowl, add a little seasoning and beat lightly with
   a fork to break the yolks.
2 Using a thick-based pan, melt the unsalted butter over a low heat and
   add the eggs.
3 Stir the eggs to prevent sticking as they cook and remove from the heat
   while there is still some liquid egg left; stir in the cream and place on
   warmed plates.
4 Sprinkle with the Parmesan and serve immediately.

Steamed spinach or chard go well with this or any egg dish.

Courgette (Zucchini) Omelette
Baked in the Oven (v) Serves 4

This unusual omelette makes a light meal – serve hot with a crisp green salad or, served cold, it becomes a useful picnic dish

1 lb/450g courgettes (zucchini), coarsely grated (shredded)
sea salt and freshly ground black pepper
4 large eggs, beaten
1 shallot or ½ small onion, chopped

1 red pepper, deseeded and finely sliced
1 clove garlic, chopped
2 tbsps chopped fresh parsley
½ cup/50g/2 oz Ricotta cheese, crumbled

1   Preheat the oven to 180°C/350°F/Gas Mark 4.
2   Place the grated courgettes (shredded zucchini) in a colander over a bowl and sprinkle with a little sea salt.
3   Leave to drain for about 20 minutes, then press out any remaining moisture using the back of a wooden spoon.
4   In a large bowl, mix together the drained courgettes (zucchini), eggs, shallot or onion, red pepper, garlic, parsley, some black pepper and the cheese.
5   Turn into an oiled 22.5-cm/9-in quiche dish or pie plate and bake for about 40 minutes until nicely puffed.
6   Scrve hot straight from the dish or allow to cool to use for a packed lunch or picnic.

Mushroom Omelette Mousseline (v) Serves 2

1 clove garlic
2 tbsps/30g/1 oz unsalted (sweet) butter
2 cups/100g/4 oz freshly sliced
   mushrooms

2 tsps olive oil
4 eggs
sea salt and freshly ground black pepper
½ tsp dried oregano

1 Use a 22.5-cm/9-in diameter omelette pan and rub the surface with
   the cut garlic clove.
2 Melt the unsalted butter and oil in the pan over a low heat and sauté
   the mushrooms for 3–4 minutes. Remove from the heat.
3 Beat the yolks and whites of the eggs separately until the yolks are
   creamy and the whites are stiff. Season the yolks with a little sea salt
   and pepper, then add the oregano and mushrooms.
4 Fold the whites into the yolks until well blended.
5 Return the omelette pan to the heat and pour in the egg mixture. Mix
   gently with a fork and cook over a moderate heat until the base of the
   omelette has set. Finish briefly under a hot grill (broiler) and slide out
   on to a warmed plate.

Mixed Vegetable Frittata (v) Serves 2

2 tbsps olive oil
1 courgette (zucchini), diced
1 celery heart, chopped
2 tomatoes, skinned, deseeded and diced

sea salt and freshly ground black pepper
4 eggs
2 tbsps Parmesan cheese, grated
1 tsp chopped fresh basil

1   Heat the oil in a 22.5-cm/9-in diameter omelette pan. Add the
    courgette (zucchini) and celery and sauté over a moderate heat until
    very slightly browned.
2   Add the tomatoes and a little seasoning and simmer for 3–4 minutes.
3   Beat the eggs with a pinch of sea salt and pepper and stir in the
    Parmesan and basil.
4   Now combine the egg mixture and the vegetables in the omelette pan
    and cook over a moderate heat until the base is browned and the
    mixture has just set. Finish quickly under a hot grill (broiler) and
    serve.

Note:
The celery heart is the inside of a bunch of celery.

Tarragon Stuffed Eggs (v) Serves 4

Tarragon is such a perfect partner for eggs that it was impossible to resist including another tarragon recipe. This one is just right for a light meal served with a salad, or for a packed meal or picnic

4 large fresh eggs	a little milk if necessary
2 tsps chopped fresh tarragon	paprika
sea salt and freshly ground black pepper	
2 tbsps cream cheese such as Mascarpone	

1 Place the eggs in a pan with enough cold water to cover; bring to the boil and simmer for 10 minutes.
2 Remove the eggs from the pan and immerse in cold water for a few minutes until they are cold. (This prevents discoloration.)
3 Shell the eggs and cut in half lengthways.
4 Remove the yolks and put into a food processor with the tarragon, a pinch of sea salt and a little ground black pepper.
5 Add the cream cheese and process just enough to blend the ingredients and give a stiff but creamy mixture. If too stiff thin down with a little milk.
6 With a teaspoon scoop out a little of the egg white and discard to enlarge the space for the filling.
7 Fill the egg whites with the yolk mixture and dust with a sprinkling of paprika.

Aubergines (Eggplants)
Stuffed with Cheese (v) Serves 4

Rose Elliot's lovely vegetable recipes have been an inspiration for many years. This is a favourite supper dish (from *Rose Elliot's Complete Vegetarian Cookbook)* and, since acquiring a food processor, the preparation time has been reduced to a minimum

4 medium aubergines (eggplants), about
   900g/2 lb total weight
1 tsp sea salt
1 onion, roughly chopped
1½ cups/175g/6 oz Cheddar cheese,
   diced

1 egg
a handful of fresh parsley
freshly ground black pepper

1 Preheat the oven to 200°C/400°F/Gas Mark 6.
2 Wash the aubergines (eggplants) and remove the stalk ends.
3 Half fill a large saucepan with cold water, add the sea salt and bring to the boil.
4 Cook the aubergines (eggplants) in the boiling water for 5 minutes until they feel barely tender when pierced with the point of a knife.
5 Drain and cool the aubergine (eggplant); split in half lengthways and scoop out the flesh, being careful not to damage the skins.
6 Arrange the skins in a lightly oiled ovenproof dish.
7 Put the aubergine (eggplant) flesh, onion, cheese, egg and parsley into a food processor and process briefly so that the texture is still coarse.
8 Add sea salt and pepper to taste and divide the mixture between the skins.
9 Bake for 30 minutes until golden brown.

A green salad and another hot vegetable, steamed runner (green) beans perhaps, go well with this dish.

Apple, Celery, Walnut and Stilton Bake (v) Serves 4

A delicious, savoury mixture

2 tbsps olive or sunflower oil
2 cups/225g/8 oz celery, very finely chopped
2 cups/225g/8 oz onions, very finely chopped
2 tsps low-salt yeast extract
1 lb/450g/1 lb eating apples, very thinly sliced

2 cups/225g/8 oz Stilton cheese, diced
2 cups/225g/8 oz walnuts, coarsely chopped
sea salt and freshly ground black pepper
⅓ cup/40g/1½ oz ground almonds
2 cups/425ml/¾ pt milk

1   Preheat the oven to 190°C/375°F/Gas Mark 5.
2   Heat the oil in a thick-based pan and add the celery and onion. Cover and cook for 20 minutes, or until tender, then stir in the yeast extract.
3   Stir in the apples and three-quarters of the Stilton, then add three-quarters of the walnuts and season to taste.
4   Mix in the ground almonds, add the milk and bring to the boil, stirring. Simmer uncovered for 2–3 minutes, stirring frequently.
5   Pour the mixture into a 1¾ L/3 pts (3¾ pts) ovenproof dish and top with the remaining cheese and walnuts. Cover with foil and cook in the oven for 1 hour.

Freezing:
Can be frozen.

Spinach, Fennel and Dolcelatte Bake (v) Serves 4

A very Mediterraneany dish!

2 tbsps olive or sunflower oil
1 lb/450g fennel, very thinly sliced
1 cup/225g/8 oz frozen spinach, thawed
2 cloves garlic, crushed (minced)
1 vegetable stock (bouillon) cube
2 tbsps tomato purée (paste)
⅓ cup/4 tbsps finely chopped fresh
    oregano or 2 tbsps dried oregano

⅓ cup/40g/1½ oz ground almonds
2 cups/225g/8 oz Dolcelatte cheese, diced
22 oz/625g canned chopped tomatoes
sea salt and freshly ground black pepper
⅓ cup/40g/1½ oz pine kernels (pignolia
    nuts)

1 Preheat the oven to 190°C/375°F/Gas Mark 5.
2 Heat the oil and cook the fennel over a gentle heat, covered, until
   tender. Add the spinach and garlic and cook for a further minute.
3 Mix in the stock (bouillon) cube and tomato purée (paste), then stir in
   the oregano, ground almonds and Dolcelatte.
4 Add the tomatoes, season to taste.
5 Transfer the mixture to a 1½ L/2½ pt (6¼ cups) ovenproof dish and
   sprinkle the pine kernels (pignolia nuts) on top. Bake uncovered for
   15–20 minutes, or until the mixture is well heated through and the
   pine kernels (pignolia nuts) golden.

Freezing:
Can be frozen.

Tomato and Courgette (Zucchini) Stuffed Mushrooms (v) Serves 4

A beautiful, savoury mushroom dish

4 large flat mushrooms approximately 11 cm/4½ in in diameter
2 tbsps olive or sunflower oil
1½ cups/175g/6 oz onion, chopped very finely
1 clove garlic, crushed
1 tsp low-salt yeast extract
1½ cups/175g/6 oz courgettes (zucchini) cut into ¼ in dice
14 oz/400g can chopped tomatoes

1½ tbsps finely chopped fresh sage or ¾ tbsp dried sage
1 tsp tamari
½ cup/50g/2 oz ground cashew nuts
½ cup/50g/2 oz cashew nuts, finely chopped
½ cup/50g/2 oz Cheddar cheese, finely grated (optional)
sea salt and freshly ground black pepper

1   Preheat the oven to 190°C/375°F/Gas Mark 5.
2   Wipe the mushroom caps and remove (but do not discard) the stalks.
3   Grease a large ovenproof dish and place the mushrooms in it stalk sides uppermost. Finely chop the stalks and put to one side.
4   Heat the oil in a large pan and fry the onion until soft. Add the garlic and yeast extract and cook for a further minute.
5   Stir in the courgettes (zucchini), tomatoes and chopped mushroom stalks and simmer until the liquid has evaporated. Add the sage and tamari, cook for a further minute, then take the pan off the heat and season to taste.
6   Mix in the ground and chopped nuts then pile the stuffing on top of each mushroom. Sprinkle with grated cheese if desired.
7   Cover with foil and bake for 20–25 minutes, until the mushrooms are tender.

Cheese and Parsnip Rissoles (v) Serves 4

A savoury cheese mixture complemented by the sweetness of parsnip

1 tbsp olive or sunflower oil
1 cup/100g/4 oz onions, very finely
   chopped
½ vegetable stock (bouillon) cube
2 tsps tamari
1½ tbsps finely chopped fresh rosemary
   or ¾ tbsp dried rosemary
1 cup/50g/2 oz mushrooms, very finely
   chopped

1½ cups/350g/12 oz parsnip, cooked
   and mashed
1 cup/100g/4 oz ground hazelnuts
1 cup/100g/4 oz ground sunflower seeds
½ cup/50g/2 oz Cheddar cheese, finely
   grated
¼ cup/3 tbsps milk

Coating
¼ cup/25g/1 oz ground sunflower seeds
¼ cup/3 tbsps very finely chopped
   hazelnuts

1 Preheat the oven to 190°C/375°F/Gas Mark 5.
2 Heat the oil and fry the onion until soft. Mix in the stock (bouillon) cube, tamari and rosemary, then add the mushrooms and cook for a further minute.
3 Remove the pan from the heat, then stir in the parsnip, hazelnuts, sunflower seeds, cheese and milk to achieve a moist consistency.
4 Divide the mixture into eight portions, shape as desired, then coat in the sunflower and hazelnut mix.
5 Place on a lightly greased baking sheet and bake for 25–30 minutes, until crisp and browned.

Serve with the ratatouille mixture and a green salad. Can also be served as a side vegetable if desired.

Freezing:
Can be frozen.

Ratatouille with a Cheesy Topping (v)

Serves 4–6 as a main course/8–10 as a vegetable

This must be one of Jackie's most popular dishes – and an absolute success at dinner parties

5 tbsps olive or sunflower oil
1 lb/450g onions, thinly sliced
4 cloves garlic, crushed
1½ cups/175g/6 oz red pepper, cut into thin strips
1½ cups/175g/6 oz green pepper, cut into thin strips
1 lb/450g courgettes (zucchini), thinly sliced

1 lb/450g aubergine (eggplant), cut into 2½-cm/1-in cubes
14 oz/400g can chopped tomatoes
1½ tbsps tomato purée (paste)
2 tbsps finely chopped fresh oregano or 1 tbsp dried oregano
sea salt and freshly ground black pepper

Cheese Sauce
¼ cup/50g/2 oz unsalted butter
2 tsps coarse grain mustard
¾ cup/75g/3 oz ground almonds

1 cup/250ml spring water
4 cups/450g/1 lb grated Cheddar cheese
sea salt and freshly ground black pepper

1 Heat the oil in a large thick-based pan. Add the onion, cover and cook until soft. Add the garlic and cook for a further minute.
2 Mix in the peppers and cook, covered, for 5 minutes, then add the aubergine (eggplant) and cook, covered, for a further 5 minutes. Repeat with the courgettes (zucchini).
3 Add the tomatoes, tomato purée (paste), oregano and seasoning. Bring to the boil and simmer, covered, for 30 minutes, stirring occasionally.
4 Preheat the oven to 190°C/375°F/Gas Mark 5.
5 Prepare the cheese sauce. Melt the unsalted butter in a pan and stir in the mustard and ground almonds. Remove the pan from the heat and add the water. Stir in the grated cheese and heat through over a low heat until all the cheese has melted. Season lightly.
6 Place the ratatouille mixture in a large ovenproof dish, pour the cheese sauce on top and bake for about 20 minutes, or until the sauce has browned.

Marinated Tofu with Arame (v) Serves 4

⅔ cup/150ml/¼ pt boiling spring water
½ cup/7g/¼ oz arame
2 tbsps light tahini
⅓ cup/4 tbsps tamari

2 tbsps cider or rice vinegar
½ cup/75g/3 oz sun-dried raisins
2 cups/450g/1 lb very firm tofu, cut into
    ½ in cubes

1   Pour the boiling water over the arame and leave to soak for at least
    20 minutes.
2   Place the tahini in a bowl. Slowly add the tamari to achieve a smooth
    mixture, then stir in the vinegar and raisins.
3   Drain the water from the arame into the tahini mixture. Very finely
    chop the arame and mix in.
4   Place the tofu in a wide-based dish, pour the tahini mixture on top,
    combine thoroughly and leave to marinate for at least 6 hours.
5   Transfer the mixture to a saucepan, bring gently to the boil, then
    simmer for 5 minutes until well heated through.

Serve with steamed green beans, carrots and a salad.

Note:
Arame is a dried sea vegetable, rich in minerals.

Walnut and Fennel Tofu Balls (v)

Serves 4 as a main course or 8 as a first course

The savouriness of walnuts and the sweetness of fennel and coconut complement each other beautifully in this dish

2 tbsps olive or sunflower oil

1½ cups/175g/6 oz onions, very finely chopped

1½ cups/175g/6 oz celery, cut into strips then thinly sliced

1 tsp low-salt yeast extract

1½ cups/175g/6 oz ground walnuts

¼ cup/3 tbsps finely chopped fresh fennel

herb or 2 tsps fennel seeds, finely chopped or ground in a pestle and mortar

⅓ cup/25g/1 oz desiccated (shredded) coconut

2 tsps tamari

1¼ cups/275g/10 oz very firm tofu

sea salt and freshly ground black pepper

Coating

⅓ cup/4 tbsps sesame seeds

⅓ cup/25g/1 oz desiccated (shredded) coconut

1   Preheat the oven to 190°C/375°F/Gas Mark 5.
2   Heat the oil in a pan and add the onion and celery. Cover and cook for 10 minutes or until soft.
3   Stir in the yeast extract then remove from the heat and add the ground walnuts, fennel, coconut and tamari.
4   Place the tofu in a food processor or blender and blend until smooth. Add to the onion mixture and season to taste.
5   Use an ice-cream scoop or spoon to scoop the mixture into 50g/2 oz amounts and shape into balls.
6   Coat in a mixture of the sesame seeds and coconut, then bake on a lightly greased baking sheet for 15–20 minutes, until the outside is golden.

Serve hot or cold as a first course with mayonnaise and a salad garnish, or for a main course with a green vegetable such as spinach, and a tomato salad.

Creamed Swiss Chard (v) Serves 4

Swiss chard is a marvellous cut-and-come again crop to grow, and makes a quickly prepared accompaniment to plain grills and roasts

2 lb/900g Swiss chard
2 tbsps unsalted (sweet) butter
⅓ cup/4 tbsps soured cream

sea salt and freshly ground black pepper
freshly grated nutmeg

1 Wash the Swiss chard and cut the chards (stems) from the leaves.
2 Cut the chards into 2½-cm/1-in lengths and steam until tender.
3 Drain and return to a pan containing the melted unsalted butter.
4 Stir in the soured cream and season with a little sea salt, pepper and nutmeg. Keep hot.
5 Meanwhile, steam the leaves for about 5 minutes. Drain and press out as much water as possible.
6 Chop roughly, place on a warmed serving dish and pour the stems and sauce over.

Creamed chard makes an excellent accompaniment to Lemon Sole with Dill (page 104).

Variation:
A little grated cheese on top transforms this into a quick supper dish, served with chopped carrots or fresh peas and a green salad.

Celeriac Purée with Herbs (v) Serves 4

1½ lb/675g celeriac, cut into even-sized
pieces
1 tbsp chopped fresh parsley
1 tsp chopped fresh oregano or ½ tsp
dried oregano

⅔ cup/150ml/¾ pt single (light) cream
sea salt and freshly ground black pepper

1 Steam the celeriac over boiling water until it feels tender when tested
   with a fork.
2 Drain well, place in a food processor and reduce to a fairly smooth
   purée.
3 Return to a pan over a low heat. Add the herbs and pour in the cream
   slowly, using a wooden spoon to beat it into the purée.
4 Season with sea salt to taste and freshly ground black pepper.

Variation:
An alternative for a light supper dish is to place the purée in a baking
dish, top with grated cheese and reheat in the oven. Serve with a crisp
green salad.

Crispy Oven Parsnips (v) Serves 4

4 medium parsnips
2 tbsps/25g/1 oz unsalted (sweet) butter
1 tbsp olive oil

1   Peel the parsnips, cut into four lengthways and remove the core. Cut
    into 5-cm/2-in lengths.
2   Steam the parsnip pieces over boiling water for about 10 minutes or
    until they feel slightly tender at the point of a knife but not soft. The
    time for this will vary according to the age of the parsnips.
3   Preheat the oven to 220°C/425°F/Gas Mark 7 while the parsnips are
    steaming. Melt the unsalted butter and oil together in a shallow
    ovenproof dish.
4   Drain the parsnips well and turn in the unsalted butter and oil
    mixture.
5   Bake the parsnips near the top of the oven for 20 minutes, when they
    should be nicely browned and crisp.

Grilled (Broiled) Nutbrown Mushrooms (v) Serves 2

This would make a quick first course or a light meal if served with a crisp green salad

6 large nutbrown mushrooms
2 tbsps chopped parsley
sea salt and freshly ground black pepper

4 cloves garlic, finely sliced
⅓ cup/4 tbsps olive oil

1   Remove the stalks from the mushrooms and chop them. Wipe the mushrooms carefully and lay in a baking dish, stalk side uppermost.
2   Mix together the parsley, seasoning and chopped mushroom stalks.
3   Press the garlic slices gently into the mushroom caps, scatter the parsley mixture evenly over and pour the olive oil over everything. Leave for a few minutes.
4   Heat the grill (broiler).
5   Grill (broil) the mushrooms under a medium heat, basting them with the cooking juices, for about 5 minutes or until they are cooked right through.

Note:
Nutbrown mushrooms are dark brown mushrooms, now available in most supermarkets.

Stir-fried Courgettes (Zucchini) with Tomato and Garlic (v) Serves 4

This dish is quick and simple to make but it cannot be kept waiting. It would be a good accompaniment to lamb cutlets (rib lamb chops) (see page 114)

1½ lb/675g courgettes (zucchini)
2–3 tbsps olive oil
3–4 cloves garlic, crushed

2–3 large tomatoes, skinned and chopped
sea salt and freshly ground black pepper

1 Wipe the courgettes (zucchini) and slice into ½cm/¼-in rounds.
2 Heat the oil in a wok or large frying pan, add the garlic and courgettes (zucchini) and stir-fry over a medium heat for 5–7 minutes.
3 Add the tomatoes and seasoning and stir-fry until the tomatoes are heated but *not* cooked.
4 Serve at once.

Courgette (Zucchini) Purée
with Fresh Basil (v) Serves 4

1½ lb/675g small courgettes (zucchini)
¼ cup/3 tbsps extra virgin olive oil
2 cloves garlic, finely chopped

2 tbsps chopped fresh basil
sea salt and freshly ground black pepper

1 Steam the courgettes (zucchini) whole for approximately 10 minutes, until tender but not soft – the skins should still be bright green.
2 Remove from the steamer and cut into small chunks.
3 Using a medium frying pan, heat 2 tbsps of the oil over a low heat. Add the garlic and cook gently for 1 minute. Add the courgettes (zucchini) and continue cooking, stirring gently, for 5 minutes.
4 Purée in a food processor with the basil and add the remaining olive oil with the motor running.
5 Reheat gently, adding sea salt and pepper to taste. If too thin, continue to cook, stirring until the purée thickens.

Creamy Carrot Purée (v) Serves 4

The beautiful colour and concentrated flavour make this purée a delicious accompaniment to chicken or fish dishes

2 lb/900g carrots, sliced
1 tbsp/15g/½ oz unsalted butter
2–4 tbsps single (light) cream
sea salt and freshly ground black pepper

1 Place the carrots in a steamer and cook gently for about 15 minutes, until tender.
2 Drain thoroughly and place in a food processor with the unsalted butter and 2 tbsps of the cream.
3 Reduce to a purée and season to taste. Add more cream if the purée is too thick.
4 Reheat gently before serving.

Creamy Basil Sauce (v) Serves 4

A beautiful sauce – lovely over vegetables for a luxurious touch to any meal!

2 tbsps olive or sunflower oil
3 cups/350g/12 oz onions, finely chopped
4 cloves garlic, crushed
½ vegetable stock (bouillon) cube
¼ cup/3 tbsps tamari

1 tbsp finely chopped fresh basil
  or ½ tbsp dried basil
¾ cup/175ml/6 fl oz double (heavy)
  cream
sea salt and freshly ground black pepper

1 Heat the oil in a thick-based pan. Add the onion and cook, covered, until soft.
2 Add the garlic, then mix in the stock (bouillon) cube, tamari and basil.
3 Stir in the cream and bring gently to the boil. Season, then simmer over a low heat for 5 minutes.

Parsnip Sauce (v) Serves 4–6

A beautiful, rich creamy sauce

¼ cup/3 tbsps olive or sunflower oil
2 lb/900g parsnips, cut into small dice
2 cups/225g/8 oz onions, finely chopped
1½ vegetable stock (bouillon) cubes
2 tsps finely chopped fresh rosemary
    or 1 tsp dried rosemary

2½ cups/570ml/1 pt spring water
⅔ cup/150ml/¼ pt double (heavy) cream
    or milk
sea salt and freshly ground black pepper

1   Heat the oil in a large pan. Add the parsnip and onion and cook, covered, for 5–10 minutes or until tender.
2   Blend in the stock (bouillon) cubes and rosemary, then add the water and cream or milk. Bring the mixture to the boil, season and simmer covered, for 5 minutes.
3   Place in a food processor or blender and blend until smooth.

Cheese Sauce for Protein Meals (v) Serves 4

¼ cup/50g/2 oz unsalted butter
2 tsps coarse grain mustard
¾ cup/75g/3 oz ground almonds
½ cup/250ml/8 fl oz spring water

4 cups/450g/1 lb mature Cheddar cheese,
   grated
sea salt and freshly ground black pepper

1 Melt the unsalted butter in a pan and stir in the mustard and ground almonds.
2 Remove the pan from the heat and add the water. Stir in the grated cheese and heat through over a low heat until all the cheese has melted. Season and serve.

Gravies and Thickenings without Flour

To Thicken Gravies and Sauces

Use potato flour – this is permissible as so little is required; 1 teaspoonful or less is often sufficient. Mix 1 teaspoon potato flour with a little cold spring water and stir into the meat juices or vegetable stock (broth). Cook at a low heat as too high a heat makes the gravy go thin again.

It is also possible to thicken very satisfactorily with ground nuts (cashews and almonds are best for this purpose as they have little effect on the flavour). Add the ground nuts as you would flour and prepare the gravy or sauce using exactly the same method – although you will find that thickening is not as quick and you will have to continue stirring for quite a while! Making sauces in this way will not produce as thick a gravy or sauce as when you use flour, but nuts are a marvellous and nutritious substitute. 100g/4 oz/1 cup ground nuts to 570m/1 pt (US 2½ cups) water, milk or stock (bouillon) gives very good results.

To Thicken Casseroles

Cook the casserole with plenty of vegetables and not too much water. When cooked, put some of the cooking liquid along with some of the vegetables into a food processor or blender and blend until thick and smooth. Return this purée to the casserole and stir in well. Alternatively, use ground nuts as above or a little potato flour.

To Make a Coating Sauce for Vegetables

Mix an egg yolk into 2 tablespoons or more of double (heavy) cream. After cooking the vegetables, reduce the cooking water to 2–3 tablespoons by fast boiling. Add the egg yolk mixture and stir gently over a low heat to prevent curdling. Season to taste.

This coating is particularly good for carrots, courgettes (zucchini), French (snap) and runner (green) beans. It not only enhances the taste of the vegetables but makes use of the nutrient-rich vegetable water which is usually thrown away.

Nut and Seed Starch-free Crackers

Reference is made throughout the protein recipe section to starch-free crackers. There are numerous excellent savoury starch-based crispbreads and crackers on the market. Starch-free crackers, however, do not appear to be available on a commercial retail basis, and in order to have an alternative to bread, crispbreads, oatcakes, etc. with protein meals, Jackie has created some starch-free recipes, as set out below.

Serve as a semi-sweet cracker with pâtés, soups, cheeses, etc., or with savoury or sweet spreads for a snack or breakfast meal. These also make an ideal base for canapés at buffets and will keep for 6–8 weeks in an airtight container.

Almond and Poppy Seed Crackers (v) Makes 15–20

Delicately flavoured crackers with a melt-in-the-mouth texture

1¾ cups/200g/7 oz ground almonds
4 tsps poppy seeds
1 tsp baking powder
½ tsp almond extract

2 tbsps/25g/1 oz unsalted butter, melted
2–3 tbsps milk
extra ground almonds for rolling out

1   Preheat the oven to 190°C/375°F/Gas Mark 5.
2   Combine the ground almonds, poppy seeds, baking powder and
    almond extract in a bowl. Mix in the melted unsalted butter, then add
    the milk and stir in using a fork.
3   Bring the mixture together with your hand to achieve a firm but moist
    dough, then roll out very thinly on a surface sprinkled with some
    ground almonds; the mixture is fairly easy to handle, but if too sticky
    sprinkle the top with some more ground almonds.
4   Cut into rounds with a 5–6cm/2–2½-in scone cutter, and use a palette
    knife to lift carefully on to a lightly greased baking sheet. Bake for 8–12
    minutes, until lightly browned and firm in texture. Leave to cool and
    harden on the sheet for a few minutes, then transfer to a wire rack to
    cool completely.

Variation:
Serve as a sweet accompaniment with ice-creams, fruit, fools (parfaits)
etc. by using 1 tsp almond extract instead of ½ tsp and cutting the dough
into fingers as well as rounds.

Caraway and Sunflower Crackers (v) Makes 15–20

The simple addition of caraway seeds to these crackers gives them a delicious flavour

2 tsps caraway seeds, roughly chopped or ground in a pestle and mortar
1 cup/100g/4 oz ground sunflower seeds
1 cup/100g/4 oz ground cashew nuts
1 tsp baking powder

2 tbsps/25g/1 oz unsalted butter, melted
2–3 tbsps milk
extra ground sunflower seeds for rolling out

1   Preheat the oven to 190°C/375°F/Gas Mark 5.
2   Combine the caraway seeds, sunflower seeds, ground cashew nuts and baking powder in a bowl. Mix in the unsalted butter, then add the milk and stir in using a fork.
3   Bring the mixture together with your hand to achieve a firm but moist dough, then roll out very thinly on a surface sprinkled with some of the extra ground sunflower seeds – the mixture is fairly easy to handle, but if too sticky sprinkle the top with some more ground sunflower seeds.
4   Cut into rounds with a 5–6-cm/2–2½-in scone cutter, and use a palette knife to lift carefully on to a lightly greased baking sheet. Bake 10–15 minutes or until browned and firm in texture. Leave to cool and harden on the sheet for a few minutes, then transfer to a wire rack to cool completely.

Cheese Crackers (v) Makes 15–20

A delicious cheesy base for savoury toppings and spreads

2 cups/225g/8 oz ground sunflower seeds
½ cup/50g/2 oz mature Cheddar cheese, finely grated
1 tsp baking powder

2–3 tbsps milk
extra ground sunflower seeds for rolling out

1   Preheat the oven to 200°C/400°F/Gas Mark 6.
2   Mix together the seeds, cheese and baking powder, then add the milk to form a dough.
3   Roll out very thinly on a surface sprinkled with some extra ground sunflower seeds – the mixture is fairly easy to handle, but if too sticky sprinkle the top with some more ground sunflower seeds.
4   Cut into rounds with a 5–6-cm/2–2½-in scone cutter, and use a palette knife to lift carefully on to a lightly greased baking sheet. Bake 10–15 minutes or until lightly browned and firm in texture. Leave to cool and harden on the sheet for a few minutes, then transfer to a wire rack to cool completely.

Variation:
Cut into small shapes and use as savoury nibbles, or form into cheese straws.

Hazelnut and Almond Crackers (v) Makes 15–20

The sweet, delicate flavour of hazelnuts makes these crackers rather special

¾ cup/75g/3 oz ground hazelnuts
1¼ cups/150g/5 oz ground almonds
1 tsp baking powder

2 tbsps/25g/1 oz unsalted butter, melted
2–3 tbsps milk
extra ground nuts for rolling out

1 Preheat the oven to 190°C/375°F/Gas Mark 5.
2 Combine the nuts and baking powder in a bowl, then mix in the unsalted butter. Add the milk and stir in using a fork.
3 Bring the mixture together with your hand to achieve a firm but moist dough, then roll out very thinly on a surface sprinkled with some of the extra ground nuts – the mixture is fairly easy to handle, but if too sticky sprinkle the top with some more ground nuts.
4 Cut into rounds with a 5–6-cm/2–2½-in scone cutter, and use a palette knife to lift carefully on to a lightly greased baking sheet. Bake 10–15 minutes or until browned and firm in texture. Leave to cool and harden on the sheet for a few minutes, then transfer to a wire rack to cool completely.

Summer Fruit Compote (v) Serves 6

This delicious fruit dish is sugar free and makes a refreshing dessert for a summer's evening dinner party or buffet. The suggested ingredients can be varied according to availability and the quantities of each fruit are a matter of taste

1 lb/450g ripe fresh apricots or
   1⅓ cups/225g/8 oz dried apricots
2½ cups/570ml/1 pt spring water
1 cup/100g/4 oz each of blackcurrants
   and redcurrants, stringed

2 cups/225g/8 oz raspberries
⅓ cup/4 tbsps apple juice concentrate

1 Skin and stone the fresh apricots, cutting each fruit into halves. Alternatively, boil the spring water and pour it over the dried apricots; leave for a few hours to plump up.

2 If using fresh apricots, pour fruit and spring water into a pan and bring to the boil; remove from heat. For the dried fruit, pour with their soaking water into a pan and bring to the boil; remove from heat.

3 Place the currants and raspberries into a bowl and pour the apricots and still hot juice over them.

4 Stir in the apple juice and set aside until cool. If possible, leave in the refrigerator for several hours or overnight for the flavours to blend.

Spiced Apple Fool (Parfait) (v) Serves 4

6 large dessert apples
⅓ cup/4 tbsps spring water
1 tbsp clear honey

½ tsp ground (powdered) cinnamon
¼ cup/3 tbsps Greek yoghurt
4 tsps double (heavy) cream

1 Peel, core and slice the apples; place in a thick-based pan with the water.
2 Add the honey and cinnamon and cook gently over a low heat until the apples are soft.
3 Remove from the heat and allow to cool.
4 Using a blender or food processor, reduce the apple mixture to a smooth purée.
5 Stir in the yoghurt, spoon into individual serving dishes or glasses and chill before serving.
6 A teaspoon of cream swirled over each fool (parfait) adds an attractive finish.

Sliced Nectarines laced with Raspberries (v) Serves 6–8

For this the fruit must be really ripe so that sugar is hardly needed. Serve with Greek yoghurt or whipped cream

6 nectarines
2 lb/1 kg raspberries
1 tbsp demerara (light brown) sugar

1   If you can obtain organically grown nectarines, then leave the skins on, but otherwise peel the fruit carefully.
2   Slice the nectarines thinly, cutting towards the stone.
3   Intermix with the raspberries in a serving bowl and sprinkle the sugar over them.
4   Cover with cling film (Saran wrap) and chill in the refrigerator until needed.

This is really a dinner party dish, and though we rarely use sugar it does enhance the flavour of the fresh fruit as no other sweetener can. Judicious use also prevents non-Hay guests from masking the flavours with over liberal use of added sugar at the table.

Autumn Fruit Compote (v) Serves 4

2 ripe dessert pears (such as Williams)
2 ripe dessert apples (such as Egremont
   Russet, Blenheim Orange or Cox's
   Orange Pippin)

⅔ cup/100g/4 oz sun-dried raisins
1¼ cups/285ml/½ pt spring water
juice of ½ lemon
2 tbsps apple juice concentrate

1   Peel and core the pears and apples and slice thinly.
2   Place the fruit and raisins in a serving bowl and pour the spring water and lemon juice over them.
3   Stir in the apple juice concentrate and leave in a cool place for the flavours to blend.

Serve with Greek yoghurt, 8% fromage frais or crème fraîche.

Spiced Pears in Red Wine (v) Serves 6–8

8 firm dessert pears
juice of ½ lemon
2 tbsps mild clear honey

¾ cup/200ml/7 fl oz spring water
½ stick cinnamon
1¼ cups/285ml/½ pt red wine

1 Preheat the oven to 160°C/325°F/Gas Mark 3.
2 Peel the pears, leaving the stalks on if possible, and put them straight into a bowl of water, with the lemon juice, to prevent discoloration.
3 Heat the honey and spring water with the cinnamon stick in a large pan and allow to simmer for 5 minutes. Remove from the heat and add the red wine.
4 Place the pears upright in a casserole and pour the wine mixture over them through a strainer.
5 Cover and bake until the pears feel soft when tested with a fork, about 30–40 minutes.
6 Remove from the oven and leave to cool.

Serve with Greek yoghurt or crème fraîche.

Baked Apple and Almond Pudding (v) Serves 4

This comforting, hot winter pudding has a crumble topping without the use of flour. Serve hot with thin cream or cold with Greek yoghurt or crème fraîche

2 lb/900g dessert apples (Ellison's Orange or Cox's are best)
2 tbsps spring water
¼ cup/50g/2 oz unsalted (sweet) butter
1–2 tbsps clear honey

¾ cup/75g/3 oz ground almonds
grated rind of 1 organic lemon
1 large egg
1 tbsp flaked (slivered) almonds

1 Preheat the oven to 180°C/350°F/Gas Mark 4.
2 Peel, core and slice the apples and put into a greased pudding dish. Add the water.
3 In a thick-based saucepan, melt the unsalted butter, add the honey and ground almonds and beat well together. Mix in the lemon rind and egg and remove from the heat.
4 Spread this mixture evenly over the apples and scatter the almonds on top.
5 Bake in the oven for 20–25 minutes.

Spiced Apricot Mousse (v) Serves 4

1⅓ cups/225g/8 oz dried apricots
½ tsp ground (powdered) nutmeg
⅓ cup/4 tbsps Greek yoghurt
flaked (slivered) almonds to decorate

1 Rinse the dried apricots, place in a bowl and add enough spring water
  to cover. Leave for 8–12 hours or overnight.
2 Place the apricots with their juice and the nutmeg in a food processor
  or blender and blend until smooth.
3 Fold the yoghurt into the apricot purée and pour into individual
  glasses.
4 Decorate with a topping of flaked (slivered) almonds.

For a richer dessert for special occasions, fold in 150ml/¼ pt/⅔ cup
whipped cream before pouring into the glasses.

Variation:
An interesting variation can be made using mangoes. Substitute the flesh
of 2 large, ripe mangoes and the juice of 1 lime for the soaked apricots.
Proceed as above, omitting the nutmeg.

Christmas Pudding (v) Serves 6–8

No food combining cookbook would be complete without Doris Grant's favourite recipe for Christmas pudding. It contains no flour or sugar and does not produce the distended feeling often experienced after eating the orthodox plum pudding

1⅓ cups/225g/8 oz whole sultanas (golden seedless raisins)

1⅓ cups/225g/8 oz sultanas (golden seedless raisins), minced

1⅓ cups/225g/8 oz large seeded raisins, minced

½ cup/75g/3 oz whole seeded raisins

16 giant prunes, soaked for 2 days until soft, then stoned (pitted) and minced

1 cup/100g/4 oz walnuts and almonds, finely chopped

1 cup/250ml/8 fl oz prune juice (from soaking prunes)

juice of 1 large orange and some grated organic orange rind

2 cups/225g/8 oz ground almonds or freshly ground hazelnuts

½ cup/125ml brandy or whisky

2 egg yolks, well beaten

brandy to serve

1 Place all the ingredients in a large mixing bowl and mix well together.
2 Grease a 1½ L/2½ pts (6¼ cups) pudding basin and transfer the mixture into it.
3 Cover well with buttered greaseproof (waxed) paper and an outer covering of foil. Steam gently for 1 hour.
4 To serve, turn out carefully on to a warmed serving dish and decorate with a sprig of berried holly. Pour a little brandy over the pudding and set alight.

The pudding can be accompanied with whipped cream flavoured with brandy.

Note:
This pudding has a rich fruity flavour, but if you prefer the traditional flavour of Christmas pudding, 1 tsp of ground mixed spice can be added to the mixture.

Freezing:
If prepared and cooked in advance, this pudding will freeze satisfactorily for 6 weeks. Allow to thaw out gradually and then steam gently for 45 minutes.

Iced Gâteau (v) Serves 8

A delicious way of eating ice-cream! Well worth the time and effort to prepare

⅔ cup/100g/4 oz dried peaches, roughly chopped
1 cup/100g/4 oz dried pineapple
1¼ cups/285ml/½ pt milk
1¼ cups/285ml/½ pt spring water
¼ cup/40g/1½ oz lexia raisins, roughly chopped

¼ cup/25g/1 oz pistachio kernels, roughly chopped
¼ cup/25g/1 oz almonds, roughly chopped
toasted flaked (slivered) almonds to decorate

1   Place the dried peaches and pineapple in separate bowls. Mix together the milk and water and soak the fruit in half the liquid overnight, or for 8–12 hours.
2   Blend each mixture separately in a food processor or blender until smooth, and put to one side.
3   Grease a 450g/1lb loaf tin (pan) and line the base with a strip of greased lining paper, long enough to overhang at both ends.
4   Spread half the peach mix over the base, then place in the freezer and leave to harden for 1 hour. Remove from the freezer and spread half the pineapple mix on top.
5   Mix together the chopped raisins and nuts and sprinkle these over the pineapple layer. Top with the remaining pineapple mix, place in the freezer for a further hour to harden, then spread the rest of the peach mix on top.
6   Return to the freezer and leave for 4 hours to set.
7   To turn out, invert on to a plate and press the base of the tin (pan); it should slip out quite quickly with the help of the lining paper.

Remove from the freezer 30–45 minutes before serving. Decorate with toasted flaked (slivered) almonds, and serve with cream or yoghurt.

Winter Fruit Compote (v) Serves 6–8

This compote based on dried fruits is a useful standby to serve after a protein meal, or on its own as a breakfast dish. It keeps well for several days in the refrigerator

⅔ cup/100g/4 oz dried apricots
⅔ cup/100g/4 oz dried pears
2 cups/100g/4 oz dried apple rings
⅔ cup/100g/4 oz sun-dried raisins
1¼ cups/285ml/½ pt spring water

2 large oranges
1 small stick cinnamon
4 cloves
1¼ cups/285ml/½ pt apple juice

1 Rinse the dried fruit in cold water and place in a large bowl.
2 Add the spring water and leave to soak overnight, or for 8–12 hours.
3 Peel the oranges and divide into segments, carefully removing all the pith.
4 Add the oranges, cinnamon, cloves and apple juice to the dried fruit. Transfer to a saucepan and gently bring to the boil.
5 Simmer for 15 minutes, remove from heat and leave to cool.
6 Remove cinnamon stick and cloves (if possible) before serving.

As a dessert this could have toasted flaked (slivered) almonds sprinkled on top. Serve with cream or Greek yoghurt.

Tofu Custard (v) Makes 570ml/1 pt (US 2½ cups)

Although not the real thing, this is a very good custard alternative and excellent for use at protein meals

2½ cups/550g/1¼ lb firm silken tofu
2 tbsps sunflower oil
2–3 tsps vanilla extract
3–4 tbsps maple syrup

1   Place all the ingredients in a food processor or blender and blend until smooth. Adjust the vanilla extract and maple syrup to suit your taste.

Serve cold as a custard topping or heat through and serve hot like custard – delicious!

Apricot Sauce (v) Makes 570ml/1 pt (US 2½ cups)

1 cup/175g/6 oz dried apricots
2½ cups/570ml/1 pt spring water

1   Place the apricots and water in a saucepan and bring to the boil.
2   Simmer for 15–20 minutes until tender, then place in a food processor
    or blender and blend until smooth. Add more water, if necessary, for
    the desired consistency.

Variation:
Use other dried fruit such as peaches or pineapple.

Suggestions for Packed Meals

Even before adopting the Hay way of eating it was usually more convenient to take a packed meal to the office, or on car or train journeys. It was cheaper, quicker (no queuing) and allowed us to eat what we enjoyed rather than what was available.

Although the sandwich is the most usual portable food, there are plenty of ways to enjoy a protein meal at your desk or when travelling, and with insulated bags and plastic containers for salads, it is easier than ever to be self-sufficient the Hay way. Here are a few suggestions:

* In winter a hot vegetable soup; in summer a chilled soup
* A container salad based on one of the light meal salads given on pages 95–99
* Slices of cold meat or chicken rolled up in lettuce leaves
* A wedge of cheese with celery and carrot sticks, cherry tomatoes, green or red pepper rings, slices of fennel root or chunks of cucumber
* A slice of cold Courgette (Zucchini) Omelette or Vegetable Frittata (pages 119 and 121), Tarragon Stuffed Eggs (page 122) or simply hard-boiled eggs with a container tomato salad, or Carrot, Apple and Raisin salad (page 85)
* Starch-free crackers with a pâté or protein spread of your choice and salad
* Cheese with apples or grapes
* Cheese and tomato and salad

To follow, pack any of the acid fruits such as apples, pears, oranges, fresh apricots or peaches, or a small container of raspberries or strawberries with Greek yoghurt. If you are still hungry, sun-dried raisins and sunflower seeds make a delicious filler.

Recipes for Starch Meals

All recipes are suitable for vegetarians

This section includes recipes for starch (carbohydrate foods) and compatible dishes to accompany them. All the recipes in the following section are compatible with each other.

Starches are essential energy-giving foods, but they should never be combined with proteins or the acid fruits (such as apples, pears, oranges, cherries, strawberries, etc. – for a full list see the Table of Compatible Foods, page 20).

The recipes in this section allow a wide choice of soups, first courses, salads, main dishes, side vegetables and desserts. Additional green vegetables and salad greens can be served with a starch meal; lists of these can be found in the Table of Compatible Foods (page 20). However, sauces and dressings for vegetables and salads should be selected only from those given in this section.

Food and Drinks that Can be Combined for a Starch Meal

Starches

All starch foods: cereals and grains (wheat, oats, barley, rye, rice, etc.) and cereal or grain products (breads, cakes, biscuits, pastas, etc.)

Dairy Products

Cream, diluted cream as a milk substitute; whole milk and yoghurt in strict moderation only

Vegetables

All green and root vegetables including potatoes and Jerusalem artichokes
Uncooked tomatoes
All salad greens and herbs

Sweet Fruits

Bananas, figs, dates, papaya, pears (if very sweet and ripe), grapes (very sweet varieties)

Note Mushrooms, nuts, oils, raisins, cream cheese, butter, cream, soured cream and egg yolks combine with all meals

Drinks

Weak tea, filter coffee in strict moderation (serve with diluted cream), dandelion coffee, herb teas, chocolate or cocoa in strict moderation (made with water and cream or diluted cream), carob drinks (made with water and cream or diluted cream)
Soft drinks: very sweet grape juice
Spring water
Alcoholic drinks: beer, lager, ale, stout, sweet wine, liqueurs, sake, whisky, gin, rum, brandy, vodka

Oatmeal Porridge Serves 2–3

This recipe first appeared in *Food Combining for Health* and is still a favourite way of preparing porridge. However, if you prefer to use oat flakes, organic grade porridge oats are now widely available

2½ cups/570ml/1 pt spring water
⅔ cup/100g/4 oz medium-cut oatmeal
pinch sea salt

1   Bring the water to the boil in a thick-based pan.
2   Stir in the oatmeal and cook at just under boiling point for 3 minutes, when the porridge will start to thicken.
3   Add a little sea salt to taste and pour into porridge bowls. As it cools slightly the porridge will thicken to the right consistency.

Serve with milk or top milk cream (half and half).

It is a good idea to sprinkle the porridge with raw oatmeal just before serving. This ensures that the porridge is well chewed rather than just swallowed – chewing is very important for starch digestion.

Banana and Papaya Cream Serves 2–3

1 papaya, approximately 450g/1 lb
   weight, peeled and finely chopped
1–2 bananas, 225g/8 oz unpeeled
   weight, sliced
½ cup/50g/2 oz ground almonds

1   Place the chopped papaya in a food processor or blender and blend
    until smooth.
2   Add the sliced banana and blend again until smooth. Stir in the
    ground almonds then chill before serving.

Serve as a breakfast dish or a dessert. It is attractive served in papaya skin
shells; cut the empty skins to fit the portion size. Delicious with grated
carob or carob powder sprinkled on top as a dessert.

Freezing:
Can be frozen, although the mixture will discolour slightly due to the
banana content.

Roasted Buckwheat and Pear Porridge Serves 2

⅔ cup/100g/4 oz roasted buckwheat
⅔ cup/100g/4 oz dried pears, chopped
1¼ cups/285ml/½ pt boiling spring water
honey or maple syrup to taste (optional)

1 Place the buckwheat and pears in a pan with the water.
2 Bring back to the boil, then cover and simmer for 7 minutes.
3 Remove from the heat and leave to stand covered for a further
   5–8 minutes, until the grains are very soft and fluffy.

Serve on its own or trickle a little honey or maple syrup on top –
it is already quite sweet though.

Banana and Fig Muesli

(Granola) Makes 450g/1 lb (US 3¹/₂ cups)

⅓ cup/50g/2 oz dried banana, cut into small pieces
⅓ cup/50g/2 oz dried figs, cut into small pieces
½ cup/50g/2 oz rolled oats
½ cup/50g/2 oz millet flakes

½ cup/50g/2 oz rye flakes
⅓ cup/50g/2 oz sun-dried raisins
½ cup/50g/2 oz hazelnuts
¼ cup/25g/1 oz pumpkin seeds
¼ cup/25g/1 oz sunflower seeds

1   Mix altogether and store in an airtight container.

Serve with boiling water or diluted cream.

Note:
For a softer textured muesli, soak in water overnight, in the fridge; then add extra water or diluted cream as desired.

Pear and Banana Crush Makes 570ml/1 pt (US 2½ cups)

10 oz/275g very ripe sweet pears, peeled
and roughly chopped
1–2 bananas, 225g/8 oz unpeeled
weight, sliced

1¼ cups/285ml/½ pt pear juice, canned
or bottled

1   Place the pears and banana in a food processor or blender and blend
    until smooth.
2   Add the pear juice and blend again; add more juice to adjust the
    consistency if desired, then chill.

Variation:
Use 225g/8 oz/1 cup drained unsweetened canned pears; these produce
a delicious flavour and are quick and easy!

Freezing:
Can be frozen although the mixture will discolour slightly due to the
banana content.

Additional Starch Breakfast Suggestions

- Banana slices sprinkled with sun-dried raisins and toasted seeds, and topped with cream or diluted cream
- Button mushrooms on toast
- Cream cheese on toast
- Egg yolks scrambled or hard-boiled on toast
- Fresh figs, dates or papaya
- Crêpes – made with egg yolks only
  Sweet – served with honey or maple syrup
  Savoury – served with cream cheese and fried mushrooms or onions
- Wholemeal (wholewheat) toast or roll with unsalted butter and a little honey
- Oat flakes soaked overnight in spring water, served with sliced banana and top milk (half and half), cream or diluted cream
- Sliced banana and fresh figs with cream or diluted cream
- Shredded wheat with top milk (half and half) cream or diluted cream

Onion and Sweetcorn Soup Serves 4

2 x 12 oz/2 x 350g cans unsweetened
   sweetcorn
2 tbsps olive or sunflower oil
1 lb/450g onions, finely chopped
1½ tsps low-salt yeast extract

2 tsps ground (powdered) ginger
2–3¼ cups/725–850ml/1¼–1½ pts
   spring water
sea salt and freshly ground black pepper

1 Blend the contents of 1½ cans sweetcorn until smooth.
2 Heat the oil in a large pan and add the onion. Cover and cook until
    soft, then stir in the blended sweetcorn, yeast extract and ginger.
3 Add the remaining sweetcorn and cook, covered, for 5 minutes.
4 Pour in the water, bring to the boil, then season, cover and simmer for
    15 minutes.

Freezing:
Can be frozen.

Hearty Vegetable Soup Serves 6

¼ cup/3 tbsps olive or sunflower oil
3 cups/350g/12 oz potatoes, cut into
small dice
3 cups/350g/12 oz leeks, cleaned weight,
thinly sliced
3 cups/350g/12 oz carrots, cut into small
dice
4 cups/450g/1 lb swede (rutabaga), cut
into small dice

2 vegetable stock (bouillon) cubes
2 tbsps finely chopped fresh parsley
2 tbsps shoyu
1 tsp freshly grated nutmeg
sea salt and freshly ground black pepper
5 cups/1L/2 pts spring water

1 Heat the oil in a large pan and add the potato. Cover and cook over a
gentle heat for 3–4 minutes. Add the remaining vegetables, cover and
cook for a further 20 minutes or until tender.
2 Mix in the stock (bouillon) cubes, then add the parsley, shoyu and
nutmeg, and season to taste.
3 Stir in the water, bring to the boil and simmer, covered, for 10 minutes.

Freezing:
Can be frozen.

Tarragon, Leek and Potato Soup Serves 6

An unusual variation on the traditional recipe

2 tbsps olive or sunflower oil
1½ lb/675g leeks, cleaned weight, thinly
  sliced
1 lb/450g potatoes, cut into small dice
2 cloves garlic, crushed
1 tbsp finely chopped fresh tarragon
  or ½ tbsp dried tarragon

½ tsp freshly grated nutmeg
1 vegetable stock (bouillon) cube
1 tbsp shoyu
¼ cup/25g/1 oz ground almonds
5 cups/1L/2 pts spring water
sea salt and freshly ground black pepper

1 Heat the oil in a large pan and add the leeks and potatoes. Cover and
  cook gently for 15–20 minutes, or until soft.
2 Stir in the garlic, tarragon and nutmeg, then mix in the stock
  (bouillon) cube, shoyu and ground almonds.
3 Add the water, bring to the boil then season and simmer, covered, for
  20 minutes.

Serve as prepared or blend for a smooth texture.

Freezing:
Can be frozen.

Pumpkin Soup Serves 4

A rich, warming soup for chilly autumn days

2 lb/1kg pumpkin flesh, measured after
    preparing as below
milk
sea salt and freshly ground black pepper

a little freshly grated nutmeg or
    1 tsp/15g/½ oz grated fresh root
    ginger
1 tbsp soured cream

1   Peel the pumpkin, remove the seeds and membrane and cut into
    chunks.
2   Steam gently until tender, then reduce to a purée in a blender or food
    processor.
3   Turn into a saucepan and add enough milk and spring water to give a
    creamy consistency. Heat through gently.
4   Season with sea salt and pepper, and add the nutmeg or ginger to
    taste.
5   Lastly, add the soured cream and serve.

Freezing:
The soup can be frozen without the soured cream.

Braised Savoury Mushrooms Serves 4

1 lb/450g button mushrooms
2 tbsps olive or sunflower oil
2 cups/225g/8 oz onions, finely chopped
½ cup/4 tbsps double (heavy) cream
1 tbsp tamari

2 tsps finely chopped fresh rosemary
    or 1 tsp dried rosemary
sea salt and freshly ground black pepper
1½ cups/75g/3 oz fresh wholemeal
    (wholewheat) breadcrumbs

1 Preheat the oven to 190°C/375°F/Gas Mark 5.
2 Wipe the mushrooms and remove stalks, then place the mushrooms
   stalk side uppermost, in an ovenproof dish.
3 Finely chop the mushroom stalks. Heat the oil and cook the onion and
   chopped mushroom together until soft. Stir in the cream, tamari and
   rosemary and simmer for a further 2–3 minutes. Season to taste.
4 Spoon the vegetable mix on top of the mushroom caps and cover the
   dish with foil.
5 Bake in the oven for 25 minutes then remove the foil, sprinkle the
   breadcrumbs on top and bake uncovered for 5–10 minutes, until the
   topping is brown and crisp.

As a first course serve with garlic bread. It is also suitable for a light lunch
or evening meal served on toast with a salad.

Corn on the Cob served with a Mixed Spice and Nutmeg Butter Serves 4

The subtle flavour of spices blend beautifully with corn – a delicious and simple dish

4 medium corn on the cob (ears of corn)
½ cup/100g/4 oz unsalted butter
2 tsps ground (powdered) mixed spice
2 tsps ground (powdered) nutmeg

1 Boil the corn cobs (ears) in plenty of water until tender, about 8–10 minutes. Meanwhile, mix together the unsalted butter and spices.
2 Serve the corn on heated plates topped with the spice butter.

Herby Haricot (Navy) Beans Serves 2

A savoury change from Boston Baked Beans!

14 oz/400g can haricot (navy) beans	2 tbsps finely chopped fresh basil
2 tsps light tahini	1 tbsp/15g/½ oz unsalted butter
2 tsps shoyu	freshly ground black pepper

1   Drain the beans and reserve 2 tablespoons of the liquid.
2   Slowly combine the tahini with the reserved liquid, then add the shoyu and basil.
3   Melt the unsalted butter in a pan, add the haricot (navy) beans and lightly fry.
4   Stir in the tahini mix, coat the beans and heat through. Season with pepper to taste.

Serve on a slice of toast or use to fill pitta breads.

Humous Serves 6–8 as a first course or 12–16 as a dip

2 x 14 oz/2 x 400g cans chick peas
(garbanzos)
3 cloves garlic, crushed
¼ cup/3 tbsps olive oil

¼ cup/3 tbsps light tahini
½ tsp paprika
1 tbsp finely grated organic lemon rind
sea salt and freshly ground black pepper

1 Drain the canned chick peas (garbanzos), and reserve the liquid.
2 Place the chick peas (garbanzos), garlic, oil, tahini and paprika in a
   food processor or blender and blend until thoroughly combined.
3 Add the lemon rind and 250ml/8 fl oz/1 cup of the reserved liquid to
   produce a very smooth, creamy consistency. Season to taste.

Present the humous in a bowl or individual ramekins, garnish with
paprika or lemon slices and serve with crudités and warmed pitta bread,
crispbreads, oatcakes, etc. It also makes an excellent jacket potato and
vegetable topping. It will keep for 4–5 days in the refrigerator in a covered
container.

Freezing:
Can be frozen but is best used within 2 months as the garlic flavour will
intensify.

Chestnut, Mushroom and Orange 'Stir' Serves 2

The sweetness and the savouriness of mushrooms combine beautifully with the sharpness of orange in this dish

1 tbsp/15g/½ oz unsalted butter
3 cups/175g/6 oz button mushrooms
1 tsp tamari
⅔ cup/75g/3 oz dried chestnuts, soaked and cooked, or 1 cup/175g/6 oz canned chestnuts, chopped

½ tsp orange rind
¼ cup/3 tbsps finely chopped fresh parsley
freshly ground black pepper

1   Melt the unsalted butter and cook the mushrooms with the tamari until tender.
2   Stir in the chestnuts, orange rind and parsley, and cook for a further 2 minutes. Season with pepper.

Serve as a light lunch or supper dish, with fresh tomato slices and toast or pitta bread.

Variation:
Grill (broil) or bake aubergine (eggplant) slices until tender, pile the chestnut mixture on top and heat through.

Papaya and Banana Slices
on a Crispy Salad Serves 4

These two fruits combine well to form an unusual first course

1 papaya, 450g/1 lb weight
2 ripe bananas, 275g/10 oz unpeeled
   weight
selection of salad leaves to garnish

1   Halve the papaya, scoop out the seeds then peel the skin and slice the
    flesh thinly in strips lengthways.
2   Peel and thinly slice the bananas.
3   Place the salad leaves on four small plates then arrange the banana
    and papaya slices on top.

Serve straightaway or very soon after preparation so that the banana does
not turn brown.

   This can also be served as a dessert in individual bowls – without the
salad leaves!

Baby Corn Cobs with Green and Red Pepper tossed in an Onion and Garlic Dressing Serves 4

A lovely combination of flavours and colours – ideal as a dinner party first course or vegetable side dish

2 tbsps olive or sunflower oil
1½ cups/175g/6 oz green pepper, deseeded and cut into thin strips
1½ cups/175g/6 oz red pepper, deseeded and cut into thin strips
4 cups/350g/12 oz baby corn cobs

sea salt and freshly ground black pepper
½ cup/125ml/4 fl oz olive oil
½ cup/50g/2 oz onions, very finely chopped
4 cloves garlic, crushed
1 tsp dried thyme

1 Heat the oil in a pan and add the peppers. Cover and cook until tender.
2 Steam or boil the baby corn cobs in a minimum of water until just tender.
3 Drain and add to the peppers, season, and continue to cook gently over a low heat.
4 Combine the olive oil, onion, garlic, thyme and seasoning and pour this mixture over the cooked vegetables. Mix thoroughly until they are well coated and heated through, then serve straightaway.

As a first course, serve on heated plates with a salad garnish.

New Potato, Spring Onion (Scallion) and Red Pepper Salad Serves 4–6

A delicious mixture of flavours

1½ lb/675g new potatoes, cooked and cut into bite-sized pieces

¼ cup/50g/2 oz spring onions (scallions), very finely chopped

1 cup/100g/4 oz red pepper, deseeded and finely diced

sea salt and freshly ground black pepper

¼ cup/3 tbsps olive oil

⅓ cup/4 tbsps finely chopped fresh parsley

1½ tsps dried oregano

1   In a large bowl mix together the potatoes, spring onions (scallions) and red pepper. Season to taste.
2   Combine the oil, parsley, oregano and seasoning, stir into the potato mixture, then refrigerate for 1 hour to allow the flavours to blend.

Rice Salad with Orange, Date and Sweetcorn Serves 4–6

The unusual combination of ingredients give this salad a unique flavour

1½ cups/225g/8 oz brown long grain rice, raw weight
7 oz/200g can sweetcorn, drained
1¼ cups/175g/6 oz dates, cooked until soft then roughly chopped

sea salt and freshly ground black pepper
¼ cup/60ml/2 fl oz olive oil
2 tsps grated organic orange rind

1 First cook the rice. Place in a saucepan with 570ml/1 pt/2½ cups spring water, season and bring to the boil. Boil hard for 5 minutes, then cover and simmer gently for 30–40 minutes, until fluffy and cooked. Transfer the rice to a large bowl and chill in the refrigerator for 20–30 minutes.
2 Remove the rice from the refrigerator, mix in the sweetcorn and dates and season to taste.
3 Mix together the oil, orange rind and seasoning, stir into the rice mixture using a fork, then refrigerate for 1 hour to allow the flavours to blend.

Minty Pea and Lemon Pasta Salad Serves 4–6

4 cups/225g/8 oz pasta shapes, cooked
3 cups/350g/12 oz frozen green peas,
   thawed and lightly steamed
sea salt and freshly ground black pepper

¼ cup/60ml/2 fl oz olive oil
1 tbsp dried mint
1 tbsp grated organic lemon rind
4 cloves garlic, crushed

1   Mix the pasta and peas together in a bowl and season to taste.
2   Combine the oil, mint, lemon rind and garlic, then pour this over the pasta mix.
3   Refrigerate for 1 hour to allow the flavours to blend.

Savoury Bread Pudding Serves 4

A delicious, quick and easy dish – and a novel way to eat bread!

2 tbsps olive oil
2½ cups/450g/1 lb onions, thinly sliced
1 vegetable stock (bouillon) cube
1 tbsp shoyu
½ cup/100g/4 oz cream cheese
4 cloves garlic, crushed
2 tsps dried thyme

2 tsps dried oregano
2 tsps dried parsley
8 slices toasted wholemeal (wholewheat)
   bread, crusts removed
⅔ cup/150ml/5 fl oz double (heavy) cream
6 large egg yolks
sea salt and freshly ground black pepper

1 Set the oven to 190°C/375°F/Gas Mark 5.
2 Heat the oil in a large pan and add the onion. Cover and cook until
   soft.
3 Stir in the stock (bouillon) cube and shoyu, then remove from the heat
   and put to one side.
4 Combine the cream cheese, garlic and herbs. Spread some of this
   mixture on each slice of toast, then cut the toast into quarters.
5 Arrange the quarters in the base of a greased 1¼L/3 pt/3¼ pt shallow
   dish. Spread some of the cooked onions on top.
6 Repeat until all the toast and onions are used up, ending with a layer
   of toast.
7 Place the cream in a measured jug and make up to 570ml/1 pt/2½
   cups with water. Transfer to a bowl, whisk in the egg yolks and season
   to taste.
8 Pour the cream and egg mixture over the toast and leave to sit for
   10 minutes.
9 Place in the oven and bake, uncovered, for 35–40 minutes, or until the
   top is browned and crunchy.

Note:
Using a shallow dish produces a lovely contrast between the moist base
and the crunchy topping.

Leek and Carrot Pasties Makes 4

The use of cream cheese, garlic and herbs in this recipe produces a lovely, savoury complement to the vegetable filling

Pastry
1½ cups/175g/6 oz plain wholemeal (all-purpose wholewheat) flour
1 cup/225g/8 oz cream cheese
½ cup/100g/4 oz unsalted butter
3 cloves garlic, crushed

2 tbsps finely chopped fresh parsley
1 tbsp finely chopped fresh thyme or ½ tbsp dried thyme
sea salt and freshly ground black pepper
beaten egg yolk to brush

Filling
2 tbsps olive or sunflower oil
1 lb/450g leeks, cleaned weight, very thinly sliced

3 cups/375g/12 oz carrots, diced
1 vegetable stock (bouillon) cube
sea salt and freshly ground black pepper

1   First make the pastry by blending together the flour, cream cheese and unsalted butter (this is speedily done in a food processor) then blend in the garlic, parsley and thyme. Season lightly.
2   Bring the mixture together to form a ball, wrap in cling film (Saran wrap) or greaseproof (waxed) paper and chill in the refrigerator for 30 minutes.
3   Heat the oil in a thick-based pan and add the leeks and carrots. Cover and cook for 15 minutes, or until tender. Mix in the stock (bouillon) cube, season to taste and leave to cool.
4   Preheat the oven to 230°C/450°F/Gas Mark 8.
5   Remove the pastry from the refrigerator, divide into four then, on a floured surface, roll out each portion to a 20-cm/8-in round. Place a quarter of the cooled mixture in the middle of each, fold the pastry over to form a pasty, press the edges together, then brush with beaten egg yolk.
6   Place on a greased baking sheet and bake for 10–15 minutes, until golden.

Aubergine (Eggplant), Mushroom and Lentil Curry Serves 4–6

With grateful thanks to Paul, one of Jackie's vegetarian cookery students, who provided the basis for the idea of this recipe

1½ cups/225g/8 oz brown basmati rice, raw weight
sea salt and freshly ground black pepper
⅓ cup/4 tbsps olive oil
2 cups/225g/8 oz onions, finely chopped
1 lb/450g aubergine (eggplant), cut into 2.5-cm/1-in cubes
2 bay leaves
1 lb/450g button mushrooms, halved
1 vegetable stock (bouillon) cube
3 green cardamoms

¼ tsp chilli powder
1 tbsp ground (powdered) ginger
1 tsp ground (powdered) cinnamon
½ tsp freshly grated nutmeg
1½ tsps ground coriander
1½ tsps ground cumin
1½ tsps turmeric
1 tbsp shoyu
1⅓ cups/225g/8 oz red lentils
3¼ cups/850ml/1½ pts boiling spring water

1 Put the rice in a saucepan with 570ml/1 pt/2½ cups spring water, season and bring to the boil. Boil hard for 5 minutes, then cover and simmer gently for 30–40 minutes, or until fluffy and cooked.
2 Meanwhile, heat the oil in a large pan and add the onion, aubergine (eggplant) and bay leaves. Cover and cook for 5 minutes. Add the mushrooms and cook a further 5–10 minutes, or until the vegetables are tender.
3 Mix in the crumbled stock (bouillon) cube and add the cardamoms.
4 Combine the chilli powder, ginger, cinnamon, nutmeg, coriander, cumin and turmeric with the shoyu, mix to a thick paste and add to the vegetables.
5 Stir in the lentils and measured water, bring the mixture to the boil, then simmer until the lentils are cooked and quite soft, about 30 minutes. Add more water while cooking if necessary, and season to taste.
6 Remove bay leaves and serve the curry in a circle of rice.

Note:
If serving six, you may want to increase the rice to 350g/12 oz/2 cups.

Cauliflower Cheese Serves 2 as a main course or 4 as a vegetable

The use of cream cheese in this recipe makes cauliflower cheese possible as a starch meal!

1¾ lb/800g cauliflower, cleaned weight, cut into medium florets
2 tbsps/25g/1 oz unsalted butter
⅓ cup/40g/1½ oz plain wholemeal (all-purpose wholewheat) flour
1 cup/225g/8 oz cream cheese

½ tsp freshly grated nutmeg
2½ cups/570ml/1 pt spring water
sea salt and freshly ground black pepper
¾ cup/40g/1½ oz fresh wholemeal (wholewheat) breadcrumbs

1   Preheat the oven to 190°C/375°F/Gas Mark 5.
2   Steam the cauliflower until tender but still slightly crunchy.
3   Melt the unsalted butter in a pan and stir in the flour to form a roux. Take the pan off the heat and mix in the cream cheese and nutmeg.
4   Gradually stir in the water to form a smooth mixture. Bring to the boil, stirring, and season to taste.
5   Place the cauliflower in a shallow ovenproof dish, pour the sauce on top and sprinkle with the breadcrumbs. Bake covered for 15 minutes and uncovered for a further 10 minutes, or until well heated through and the breadcrumbs are browned and crispy on top.

Freezing:
Can be frozen.

Onion and Oregano Flan Serves 4–6

The sweetness of onions and the round, strong flavour of oregano make a beautiful combination – this is always a favourite dish

Pastry
½ cup/50g/2 oz plain wholemeal (all-purpose wholewheat) flour
½ cup/50g/2 oz self-raising wholemeal flour (all-purpose wholewheat flour sifted with ½ tsp baking powder)

½ cup/50g/2 oz walnuts, finely chopped
pinch sea salt
6 tbsps/75g/3 oz unsalted butter
¼ cup/60ml/2 fl oz ice-cold spring water

Filling
2 tbsps olive or sunflower oil
1¼ lb/550g onions, thinly sliced
4 cloves garlic, crushed
1 vegetable stock (bouillon) cube
2 tbsps finely chopped fresh oregano
   or 1 tbsp dried oregano

sea salt and black pepper
¼ cup/60ml/2 fl oz double (heavy) cream
⅓ cup/90ml/3 fl oz spring water
3 large egg yolks

1 First make the pastry. Sift the flours into a bowl. Add a pinch of sea salt, then gently rub the unsalted butter into the flour until the mixture resembles fine breadcrumbs, and mix in the walnuts. Add the water, and combine to achieve a moist but not too sticky dough. Cover and chill in the refrigerator for 30 minutes.
2 Preheat the oven to 200°C/400°F/Gas Mark 6.
3 Roll out the pastry to fit a 22.5-cm/9-in flan dish and bake blind for 10–15 minutes, or until lightly golden. Remove, and reduce the heat to 190°C/375°F/Gas Mark 5.
4 Heat the oil in a large pan and add the onion. Cover and cook over a gentle heat until very soft.
5 Mix in the garlic, stock (bouillon) cube, oregano and seasoning. Leave the mixture to cool slightly, then place in the pastry case.
6 Whisk together the cream, water and egg yolks, pour over the onion mix and bake for 25–35 minutes, until set and lightly browned.

Broccoli and Courgette (Zucchini) Rice baked in a Leek and Nutmeg Sauce Serves 6

2 cups/350g/12 oz long grain brown rice,
   raw weight
1 vegetable stock (bouillon) cube
3¾ cups/850ml/1½ pts spring water
sea salt and freshly ground black pepper
⅓ cup/4 tbsps olive oil

1 lb/450g broccoli, finely chopped
1 lb/450g courgettes (zucchini), very
   finely diced
2 bay leaves
2 tbsps tamari

Leek and Nutmeg Sauce
2 tbsps olive oil
1 lb/450g leeks, finely chopped
½ vegetable stock (bouillon) cube
2 tsps freshly grated nutmeg

⅓ cup/40g/1½ oz plain wholemeal (all-
   purpose wholewheat) flour
2½ cups/570ml/1 pt spring water
sea salt and black pepper

1 First cook the rice. Place in a saucepan with the stock (bouillon) cube, water and seasoning. Bring to the boil, boil hard for 5 minutes then cover and simmer over a gentle heat for 30–40 minutes, until fluffy and tender.
2 Meanwhile, heat the oil in a large pan and add the broccoli, courgettes (zucchini) and bay leaves. Cover and cook gently until tender, about 10–15 minutes. Stir in the tamari, cook for a further minute and season to taste.
3 Prepare the sauce, heating the oil and cooking the leeks in a covered pan until tender.
4 Mix in the crumbled stock (bouillon) cube and nutmeg, then stir in the flour. Remove the pan from the heat and slowly add the water, stirring continuously to prevent any lumps forming.
5 Return the pan to the heat and bring gently to the boil, stirring until the sauce thickens. Simmer for 5 minutes and season to taste.
6 Preheat the oven to 190°C/375°F/Gas Mark 5.

7   Grease a lasagne dish or similar measuring approximately 20 x 30cm/ 8 x 12in. Spread one third of the cooked rice over the bottom, top with a third of the vegetable mixture and then pour over a quarter of the leek sauce. Do this three times, finishing up with a thicker layer of sauce.

8   Leave the dish to stand for 20–30 minutes to allow the sauce to be absorbed, then cook covered for 30 minutes and uncovered for 10 minutes, or until the surface is lightly browned and slightly crunchy.

Serve with a tomato and onion salad to achieve an effective colour contrast.

Cheesy Carrot and Potato Pie Serves 6

A delicious and hearty pie

Pastry
1 cup/100g/4 oz self-raising wholemeal
   flour (all-purpose wholewheat flour
   sifted with 1 tsp baking powder)
1 cup/100g/4 oz plain wholemeal (all-
   purpose wholewheat) flour

pinch sea salt
½ cup/100g/4 oz unsalted butter
⅓ cup/90ml/3 fl oz ice-cold spring water

Filling
1¾ lb 800g/1¾ lb carrots, cut into
   2.5cm/1-in cubes
1¾ lb 800g/1¾ lb potatoes, cut into
   2.5cm/1-in cubes
2 tsps finely chopped fresh thyme
   or 1 tsp dried thyme

2 tsps finely chopped fresh rosemary
   or 1 tsp dried rosemary
2 tbsps finely chopped fresh parsley
1 cup/225g/8 oz cream cheese
sea salt and freshly ground black pepper

1   Make the pastry by sifting the flours into a bowl, adding back any
    separated bran. Mix in a pinch of sea salt, then gently rub the unsalted
    butter into the flour until the mixture resembles fine breadcrumbs.
    Add the water, and combine to achieve a moist but not too sticky
    dough. Cover and chill for 30 minutes.
2   Preheat the oven to 200°C/400°F/Gas Mark 6.
3   Roll out the pastry to fit a 25-cm/10-in flan dish and bake blind for
    10–15 minutes, or until lightly golden and firm to the touch. Remove,
    and reduce the oven temperature to 190°C/375°F/Gas Mark 5.
4   Steam the carrots and potatoes together until just tender, then put to
    one side to cool.
5   Mix the herbs with the cream cheese and season to taste. Add to the
    potatoes and carrots and combine thoroughly so that the vegetables
    are well coated.
6   Pile the carrots and potato mix into a mound in the pastry case. Bake
    uncovered for 20–25 minutes, until the top is lightly browned and firm.

Courgette and Aubergine Flan Serves 6–8

Pastry
1 cup/100g/4 oz self-raising wholemeal
    flour (all-purpose wholewheat flour
    sifted with 1 tsp baking powder)
1 cup/100g/4 oz plain wholemeal (all-
    purpose wholewheat) flour

pinch sea salt
½ cup/100g/4 oz unsalted butter
⅓ cup/90 ml/3 fl oz ice-cold spring water

Filling
3 cups/350g/12 oz courgettes (zucchini),
    cut into 2.5-cm/1-in cubes
3 cups/350g/12 oz aubergine (eggplant),
    cut into 2.5-cm/1-in cubes
2 tsps caraway seeds, chopped or crushed

4 cloves garlic, crushed
2 tbsps shoyu
⅓ cup/90ml/3 fl oz double (heavy) cream
¾ cup/200ml/7 fl oz spring water
4 large egg yolks
sea salt and freshly ground black pepper

1   Make the pastry by sifting the flours into a bowl, adding back any
    separated bran. Add a pinch of sea salt, then gently rub the unsalted
    butter into the flour until the mixture resembles fine breadcrumbs.
    Add the water, and combine to achieve a moist but not too sticky
    dough (if too moist add extra flour). Cover and chill for 30 minutes.
2   Preheat the oven to 200°C/400°F/Gas Mark 6.
3   Roll out the pastry to fit a 25-cm/10-in flan dish and bake blind for
    10–15 minutes, until lightly golden.
4   Steam the courgettes (zucchini) and aubergine (eggplant) until tender.
    Drain thoroughly.
5   Add the caraway seeds, garlic and shoyu, and place the filling in the
    part-cooked pastry base.
6   Whisk together the cream, water and egg yolks, season and pour over
    the vegetable mix.
7   Place in the oven and cook for 35–40 minutes, or until the mixture is
    set.

Leek and Mushroom Quiche Serves 4–6

A full-flavoured quiche, lovely hot or cold

Pastry
1 cup/100g/4 oz self-raising wholemeal
   flour (all-purpose wholewheat flour
   sifted with 1 tsp baking powder)
1 cup/100g/4 oz plain wholemeal (all-
   purpose wholewheat) flour

pinch sea salt
½ cup/100g/4 oz unsalted butter
⅓ cup/90 ml/3 fl oz ice-cold spring water

Filling
2 tbsps olive oil
1 lb/450g leeks, cleaned weight, thinly
   sliced
4 cups/225g/8 oz mushrooms, thinly
   sliced

1 vegetable stock (bouillon) cube
1 tbsp tamari
1 tbsp dried marjoram
sea salt and freshly ground black pepper
⅔ cup/60g/2½ fl oz double (heavy) cream
3 large egg yolks

1   Make the pastry in the usual way (see page 193).
2   Preheat the oven to 200°C/400°F/Gas Mark 6.
3   Roll out the pastry to fit a 25-cm/9–10-in flan dish and bake blind for
    10–15 minutes, or until lightly golden and firm to the touch.
4   Heat the oil in a large pan and add the leeks. Cover and cook until
    tender, then add the mushrooms and cook uncovered for a further 3–4
    minutes, or until tender. Mix in the stock (bouillon) cube, tamari and
    marjoram. Season to taste, then put the mixture to one side to cool.
5   Once cool, place the mixture in the part-cooked pastry base.
6   Whisk together the cream and egg yolks, making the solution up to
    285ml/10 fl oz/1⅓ cups with water. Pour over the vegetable mix.
7   Bake in the oven for 30–35 minutes, or until the top is browned and
    the filling set.

Lentil and Celery Loaf with a Leek Filling Serves 6–8

A delicious savoury loaf mix, beautifully offset by the sweetness of the leek filling

¾ cup/150g/5 oz brown lentils
2 cups/425ml/¾ pt spring water
⅓ cup/4 tbsps olive or sunflower oil
3 cups/350g/12 oz leeks, cleaned weight, very thinly sliced
2 bay leaves
1½ tbsps light tahini
1½ cups/175g/6 oz onions, finely chopped
3 cups/350g/12 oz celery, very finely chopped

2 cloves garlic, crushed
1 vegetable stock (bouillon) cube
1 tbsp finely chopped fresh sage
  or ½ tbsp dried sage
2 tsps finely chopped fresh thyme
  or 1 tsp dried thyme
1 tsp finely grated organic lemon rind
2 cups/100g/4 oz fresh wholemeal (wholewheat) breadcrumbs
sea salt and freshly ground black pepper

1   Rinse the lentils then cook in the water over a gentle heat until soft and all liquid absorbed.
2   Preheat the oven to 190°C/375°F/Gas Mark 5.
3   Heat 2 tbsps oil and gently cook the leeks in a covered pan with the bay leaves until very soft. Remove the bay leaves, stir in the tahini, season and put to one side.
4   Heat the remaining oil in a separate pan and add the onion and celery. Cover and cook until very soft, then add the garlic and cook for a further 2–3 minutes. Combine with the cooked lentils then mix in the stock (bouillon) cube, herbs, lemon rind and breadcrumbs. Season well.
5   Grease and line a 900g/2 lb loaf tin (pan) with greased lining paper long enough to overhang at both ends.
6   Place 350g/12 oz of the lentil mixture in the base and smooth over, place the leek mixture on top and finish with the remaining lentils.
7   Bake uncovered for 30–40 minutes, or until browned and firm to the touch. Serve hot or cold.

Vegetable and Borlotti (Pinto) Bean Lasagne with a Crunchy Breadcrumb Topping Serves 6

The strong, savoury taste of borlotti (pinto) beans adds a rich flavour to this lasagne

Base

2 tbsps olive or sunflower oil

1½ cups/175g/6 oz onions, very finely chopped

1½ cups/175g/6 oz courgettes (zucchini), finely diced

1½ cups/175g/6 oz carrots, finely diced

1½ cups/175g/6 oz celery, very finely chopped

2 cloves garlic, crushed

1 vegetable stock (bouillon) cube

2 tbsps shoyu

2 tbsps finely chopped fresh oregano or 1 tbsp dried oregano

2 tbsps finely chopped fresh thyme or 1 tbsp dried thyme

14 oz/400g can borlotti (pinto) beans

sea salt and freshly ground black pepper

6 oz/175g no-precook wholemeal (wholewheat) lasagne sheets

1 cup/50g/2 oz fresh wholemeal (wholewheat) breadcrumbs

Sauce

¼ cup/40g/1½ oz unsalted butter

½ cup/50g/2 oz plain wholemeal (all-purpose wholewheat) flour

pinch paprika

1¼ cups/275g/10 oz cream cheese

3 cups/725ml/1¼ pts spring water

sea salt and freshly ground black pepper

1   Heat the oil in a large pan and add the prepared vegetables. Cover and cook for 15 minutes, or until soft, then add the garlic, stock (bouillon) cube, shoyu, oregano and thyme.

2   Drain the borlotti (pinto) beans and reserve the liquid. Add the beans to the vegetable mix, combine well and season. Put the mixture to one side.

3   Preheat the oven to 200°C/400°F/Gas Mark 6.

4   Make the sauce by melting the unsalted butter in a pan and stirring in the flour and paprika. Take the pan off the heat and mix in the cream cheese to form a smooth paste.

5 Add spring water to the borlotti (pinto) bean liquid to make up to 725ml/1¼ pts (US 3 cups). Add to the cream cheese mix, stirring continuously to prevent lumps forming. Return the pan to the heat and, stirring constantly, gently bring to the boil until the mixture thickens. Season well.

6 Place a layer of the vegetable mixture in the base of a 1¾ L/3 pts/7½ cup dish (a deep square or rectangular dish is ideal), top with a layer of lasagne sheets, and then spread over a little sauce.

7 Repeat the layers, leaving enough sauce to finish with a thick layer. Bake uncovered in the oven for 30 minutes, then sprinkle with the breadcrumbs and bake for a further 10 minutes, or until the topping is crisp and browned and the lasagne is tender.

Freezing:
Can be frozen.

Vegetable Stroganoff Serves 4

1½ cups/225g/8 oz long grain brown rice, raw weight

2½ cups/570ml/1 pt spring water

sea salt and freshly ground black pepper

2 tbsps olive oil

2 cups/225g/8 oz onions, cut into semi-circle slices

2 cloves garlic, crushed

2⅔ cups/225g/8 oz baby corn cobs, halved lengthways

2 cups/225g/8 oz red pepper, cut into strips

6 cups/350g/12 oz button mushrooms, halved

1 vegetable stock (bouillon) cube

1½ tsps ground cumin

1½ tsps ground coriander

¼ cup/25g/1 oz plain wholemeal (all-purpose wholewheat) flour

1¼ cups/285ml/½ pt soured cream

1 Put the rice in a saucepan with the water and seasoning and bring to the boil. Boil hard for 5 minutes, then cover and simmer gently for 30–40 minutes, or until fluffy and cooked.

2 Meanwhile, heat the oil in a large pan and add the onion, garlic, baby corn cobs and red pepper. Cover and cook for 5 minutes over a gentle heat. Add the mushrooms and cook for a further 5 minutes, or until the vegetables are tender.

3 Mix in the crumbled stock (bouillon) cube and spices, then stir in the flour.

4 Take the pan off the heat, add the cream, return to the heat and bring gently to the boil, stirring continuously.

5 Simmer for 5 minutes, season to taste and serve on a bed of rice.

Mushroom and Tarragon Bake

Serves 4 as a main course or 6–8 as a first course

A lovely rich mushroom layer on top of a crisp golden cornmeal base

Topping
2 tbsps olive or sunflower oil

3 cups/175g/6 oz mushrooms, thinly sliced

1 cup/100g/4 oz onions, finely chopped

2 cloves garlic, crushed

1½ tbsps tamari

1½ tbsps finely chopped fresh tarragon or ¾ tbsp dried tarragon

⅓ cup/4 tbsps plain wholemeal (all-purpose wholewheat) flour

½ cup/125ml/4 fl oz spring water

sea salt and freshly ground black pepper

Base
1 cup/100g/4 oz plain wholemeal (all-purpose wholewheat) flour

¾ cup/100g/4 oz cornmeal flour

4 tsps baking powder

pinch sea salt

¼ cup/50g/2 oz unsalted butter

½ cup/125ml/4 fl oz spring water

1 Preheat the oven to 200°C/400°F/Gas Mark 6.
2 Heat 1 tbsp oil and sauté the sliced mushrooms until tender. Remove from the pan and put to one side.
3 Add the remaining oil to the pan and fry the onion until soft. Stir in the chopped mushrooms, garlic, tamari and tarragon, and cook for a further 2–3 minutes.
4 Stir in the flour for a minute, remove the pan from the heat and stir in the water. Mix in the sliced mushrooms and season.
5 Make the base. Combine the flours, baking powder and sea salt in a bowl, and rub in the unsalted butter. Stir in the water using a fork, then bring the mixture together to achieve a firm but moist dough.
6 Roll out on a floured surface to line the base of a 25-cm/10-in greased loose-bottomed flan tin (pie pan), and spread the mushroom mixture on top of the corn base.
7 Bake for 10 minutes uncovered, then 5 minutes covered, until the base is crisp and golden. Serve hot or cold.

Bean Jar Serves 4–6

This variation on a traditional Guernsey recipe is always a guaranteed success with its delicious combination of beans and herbs – well worth the lengthy cooking time

⅔ cup/100g/4 oz butter (lima) beans
1⅓ cups/225g/8 oz kidney beans
⅔ cup/100g/4 oz haricot (navy) beans
1 lb/450g carrots, roughly sliced
1 lb/450g onions, sliced
⅔ cup/100g/4 oz red lentils

2 vegetable stock (bouillon) cubes
¼ cup/3 tbsps dried parsley
¼ cup/3 tbsps dried thyme
1 tbsp dried rosemary
sea salt and freshly ground black pepper

1 Soak all the beans overnight or for 8–12 hours in cold water to cover. Drain.
2 Preheat the oven to 200°C/400°F/Gas Mark 6.
3 Place all the ingredients except the sea salt and pepper in a very large casserole or ovenproof dish and stir well together.
4 Add sufficient spring water to cover, then place in the oven and bring to the boil.
5 Allow to boil for 20 minutes, then reduce the oven temperature to 120°C/250°F/Gas Mark ½ and leave to simmer for a minimum of 4 hours – adding more boiling water as necessary.
6 Remove from the oven and season to taste.

Bean Jar is a substantial dish and should be eaten as a main course with wholemeal (wholewheat) bread. It can also be served as a jacket potato topping, crêpe filling or as a bake with a savoury crumble topping.

Lentil and Herb Burgers Makes 8

A delicious, savoury recipe – popular with adults and children alike!

2 cups/350g/12 oz brown lentils
3¼ cups/850ml/1½ pts spring water
2 tbsps olive or sunflower oil
3 cups/350g/12 oz onions, finely chopped
4 cloves garlic, crushed
2 vegetable stock (bouillon) cubes
2 tbsps finely chopped fresh oregano
    or 1 tbsp dried oregano

1 tbsp finely chopped fresh sage
    or ½ tbsp dried sage
4½ cups/250g/9 oz wholemeal
    (wholewheat) breadcrumbs
sea salt and freshly ground black pepper

1   Cook the lentils in the water until soft and mushy and all the liquid
    has been absorbed.
2   Preheat the oven to 190°C/375°F/Gas Mark 5.
3   Heat the oil in a large pan and add the onion. Cover and cook until
    soft, then add the garlic and cook for a further minute.
4   Mix in the stock (bouillon) cubes and herbs, then take the pan off the
    heat and mix in the cooked lentils and 175g/6 oz/3 cups of the
    breadcrumbs. Season to taste.
5   Divide the mixture into eight portions and mould into burger shapes
    (the mixture will be fairly sticky, but once baked will become less
    moist).
6   Finally, toss each burger in the remaining breadcrumbs, place on a
    lightly greased baking sheet and bake for 15–20 minutes until the
    coating is crisp and golden.

Serve in a bun with salad garnish and low-fat oven fries; or with fried
onions, peas and low-fat oven fries.

Freezing:
Can be frozen.

Courgette (Zucchini) and Red Pepper Pizza

A tasty Hay alternative to the traditional pizza!

1¼ cups/275g/10 oz cream cheese
2 tbsps dried oregano
1 tbsp dried thyme
2 cloves garlic, crushed
2 tbsps olive oil
2 cups/350g/12 oz onions, thinly sliced
2 cups/350g/12 oz red peppers, diced

2 cups/350g/12 oz courgettes (zucchini),
thinly sliced
1 vegetable stock (bouillon) cube
1½ tbsps shoyu
freshly ground black pepper
4 wholemeal (wholewheat) pitta breads

1 Preheat the oven to 200°C/400°F/Gas Mark 6.
2 Combine the cream cheese, herbs and garlic. Set to one side.
3 Heat the oil in a large pan and add the onion and pepper. Cover and cook until soft.
4 Mix in the courgettes (zucchini) and cook, covered, until tender.
5 Stir in the stock (bouillon) cube and shoyu; season with black pepper to taste.
6 Combine the cream cheese mixture with the vegetables, stirring well.
7 Place the pitta breads on a baking sheet and spread each one with a quarter of the cream cheese and vegetable mixture. Bake uncovered for 10–15 minutes until heated through.

Note:
Do not bake these pizzas for too long, as the pitta base will become too crisp and difficult to eat!

Freezing:
The topping can be frozen and the pizzas made up after thawing.

Macaroni Cheese Serves 4

Another Hay version of a popular dish – and just as good as the traditional recipe

2 cups/225g/8 oz wholemeal (wholewheat) macaroni
2 tbsps olive oil
2 cups/350g/12 oz onions, thinly sliced
1 vegetable stock (bouillon) cube
2 tsps dried oregano

⅓ cup/40g/1½ oz plain wholemeal (all-purpose wholewheat) flour
1 cup/225g/8 oz cream cheese
2½ cups/570ml/1 pt wholemeal (wholewheat) breadcrumbs
sea salt and freshly ground black pepper

1 Preheat the oven to 200°C/400°F/Gas Mark 6.
2 Cook the macaroni in plenty of fast-boiling water for 10–12 minutes, until just tender. Drain thoroughly and put to one side.
3 Heat the oil in a large pan and add the onion. Cover and cook until tender.
4 Mix in the stock (bouillon) cube and oregano, then add the flour and cook for 1 minute.
5 Stir in the cream cheese until well combined, then remove from the heat. Slowly add the water, stirring continuously to prevent any lumps forming.
6 Return to the heat, season then bring slowly to the boil. Simmer gently, uncovered, for 5 minutes.
7 Place the cooked macaroni in a 1½ L/2½ pt/6¼ cup dish, pour the sauce over, then sprinkle the breadcrumbs on top.
8 Bake in the oven for 15–20 minutes or until the topping is golden and crunchy.

Freezing:
Can be frozen.

Spaghetti Mushroom Bolognese Serves 4

An extremely popular alternative to traditional spaghetti Bolognese

2 tbsps olive oil
1⅔ cups/275g/10 oz onions, finely
chopped
1⅔ cups/275g/10 oz carrots, cut into
small dice
2 cloves garlic, crushed
2 lb/900g mushrooms, very finely
chopped
1 vegetable stock (bouillon) cube

2 tbsps tamari
2 tsps dried thyme
2 tsps dried oregano
2 tsps plain wholemeal (wholewheat)
flour
sea salt and freshly ground black pepper
8 oz/225g wholemeal (wholewheat)
spaghetti

1   Heat the oil in a large pan and add the onion, carrot and garlic. Cover
    and cook until soft. Add the mushrooms.
2   Mix in the stock (bouillon) cube, tamari and the herbs.
3   Stir in the flour, then season to taste. Cover and simmer gently for
    10–15 minutes.
4   Meanwhile, cook the pasta in plenty of fast-boiling water for 10–12
    minutes, until just tender. Drain thoroughly, transfer to a warmed
    serving dish and top with the 'Bolognese' sauce. Serve at once.

Freezing:
The sauce can be frozen, then used as required once thawed.

Curried Jacket Potatoes Serves 4

A simple but tasty way to serve jacket potatoes

4 large jacket potatoes, approximately
    275g/10oz each in weight
¼ cup/3 tbsps olive or sunflower oil
1 lb/450g onions, finely chopped
1 tbsp medium curry powder

⅔ cup/8 tbsps finely chopped fresh
    parsley
⅓ cup/4 tbsps double (heavy) cream
    (optional)
sea salt and freshly ground black pepper

1   Bake the potatoes until tender, using your favourite method.
2   Increase the oven temperature if necessary to 190°C/375°F/
    Gas Mark 5.
3   Heat the oil in a large pan and cook the onion with the curry powder,
    covered, until soft. Add the parsley and cream if using.
4   Cut each potato in half lengthways and scoop out, leaving enough
    potato in the skin to form a shell; put these to one side then add the
    scooped out potato to the onion and curry mix. Season to taste.
5   Combine thoroughly, pile back into the reserved shells and place on a
    lightly greased baking sheet.
6   Cover loosely with foil and cook in the oven for 20–30 minutes, until
    well heated through.

Too-Tired-to-Cook Rice Serves 4

There are many good rice and vegetable recipes suitable for the Hay System, but the title of this recipe from *Rose Elliot's Complete Vegetarian Cookbook* (Collins, 1985) says it all! It has saved the day for us on innumerable occasions over the years, when coming home late to face the task of preparing a meal from scratch really was the last thing we felt like doing! You can put the rice on to cook and then go away to recover for about 30 minutes; the last part of the recipe can be prepared during the final 10 minutes of the cooking time

1½ cups/225g/8 oz long grain brown rice, raw weight
2½ cups/570ml/1 pt spring water
1 tsp sea salt

4 cups/225g/8 oz button mushrooms
1 tbsp/15g/½ oz unsalted butter
½ cup/50g/2 oz sunflower seeds
shoyu

1   Put the rice, water and sea salt into a pan and bring to the boil. Boil hard for 5 minutes, then cover the pan with a well fitting lid and turn the heat down to its lowest point. Leave to cook for 30 minutes.
2   Fry the mushrooms in the unsalted butter.
3   When the rice is cooked, fork up and add the sunflower seeds.
4   Serve with the mushrooms and their juices poured over and add a sprinkling of shoyu.

Crusty wholemeal (wholewheat) rolls and butter plus a crisp green salad complete this easily assembled supper.

New Potatoes tossed in Garlic and Herb Butter Serves 4

A truly delicious way to serve new potatoes – another dinner party favourite

1½ lb/675g new potatoes, cleaned
¼ cup/50g/2 oz unsalted butter
6 cloves garlic, very finely chopped
2 tsps finely chopped fresh rosemary
   or 1 tsp dried rosemary

1 tsp finely chopped fresh thyme
   or ½ tsp dried thyme
sea salt and freshly ground black pepper

1   Steam the potatoes until tender, about 15–20 minutes.
2   Melt the unsalted butter in a large pan and gently sauté the garlic with the herbs until lightly golden. Season.
3   Add the potatoes to the pan and turn thoroughly until well coated in the garlic and herbs and heated through.

Humous Green Beans Serves 4

An unusual combination, but one that works very well to produce an extremely tasty vegetable dish

1 lb/450g thin green beans, trimmed
½ quantity Humous (page 178)
sea salt and freshly ground black pepper

1   Preheat the oven to 190°C/375°F/Gas Mark 5.
2   Steam the green beans until tender, then place in the base of an ovenproof dish.
3   Spread the humous on top, season lightly and bake uncovered for 15 minutes or until well heated through.

Humous is equally good on other vegetables – especially greens.

Sesame Potatoes Serves 4–6

Sesame seeds give a pleasant crunchy texture to this dish

1½–2 lb/675–900g potatoes, cut into
   large dice
¼ cup/25g/1 oz sesame seeds, toasted
sea salt and freshly ground black pepper

1   Boil the potatoes until tender.
2   Drain off any excess water, toss in the sesame seeds and season.

We always enjoy a mashed version of this recipe – simply mash the
potatoes until smooth, adding a little unsalted butter to achieve this, then
stir in the toasted seeds.

Cream Cheese Sauce Serves 4–6

Cream cheese is a useful addition to the food combining diet, making a
starch cheese sauce possible

2 tbsps unsalted butter
6 tbsps/40g/1½ oz plain wholemeal (all-
purpose wholewheat) flour

1 cup/225g/8 oz cream cheese
2½ cups/570ml/1 pt spring water
sea salt and freshly ground black pepper

1   Melt the unsalted butter and stir in the flour to form a roux.
2   Take the pan off the heat and mix in the cream cheese.
3   Gradually stir in the water to form a smooth mixture, then bring gently
    to the boil, stirring continuously, until the mixture thickens. Season to
    taste.

Freezing:
Can be frozen.

Red Pepper Sauce Serves 6

1 tbsp olive or sunflower oil
½ cup/50g/2 oz onion, very finely
    chopped
½ cup/50g/2 oz celery, very finely
    chopped
1½ cups/175g/6 oz red pepper, deseeded
    and finely diced
1 tsp low-salt yeast extract

1 tsp finely chopped fresh thyme
    or ½ tsp dried thyme
1 tsp finely chopped fresh marjoram
    or ½ tsp dried marjoram
6 tbsps/40g/1½ oz plain wholemeal (all-
    purpose wholewheat) flour
2½ cups/570ml1 pt spring water
sea salt and freshly ground black pepper

1   Heat the oil in a pan and add the onion, celery and red pepper. Cover
    and cook over a gentle heat for 10–15 minutes, or until soft.
2   Mix in the yeast extract and herbs, then stir in the flour and remove
    the pan from the heat.
3   Slowly add the water, stirring all the time to prevent any lumps
    forming, then return the pan to the heat. Bring to the boil, stirring
    continuously until the sauce thickens, then season.

Serve as prepared or place in a food processor or blender and blend until
smooth; eat with nut loaves, burgers, bakes, pies, crêpes, etc.

Freezing:
Can be frozen.

Parsley Sauce Serves 6

¼ cup/50g/2 oz unsalted butter
4 fresh bay leaves
2 cloves garlic, crushed
¼ tsp paprika
½ vegetable stock (bouillon) cube
¾ cup/9 tbsps finely chopped fresh
    parsley

½ cup/50g/2 oz plain wholemeal (all-
    purpose wholewheat) flour
2½ cups/570ml/1 pt spring water
sea salt and freshly ground black pepper

1   Melt the unsalted butter in a pan, add the bay leaves, garlic and
    paprika, and cook for 1–2 minutes. Mix in the half stock (bouillon)
    cube then add the parsley.
2   Stir in the flour, then remove the pan from the heat and slowly add the
    water, stirring all the time to prevent any lumps forming.
3   Return the pan to the heat and bring to the boil, stirring continuously
    until the sauce thickens. Season to taste.

Serve with main course dishes or as a vegetable topping. Delicious with
potatoes, and it makes a tasty alternative to cauliflower cheese when
served with cauliflower.

Freezing:
Can be frozen.

Vegetarian Gravy Serves 4–6

A quick, easy recipe for a gravy substitute

2 tbsps/25g/1 oz unsalted butter
6 tbsps/40g/1½ oz plain wholemeal (all-purpose wholewheat) flour
¼ cup/25g/1 oz ground almonds
1 tsp dried thyme

1 tsp dried parsley
1 tsp tamari
1 vegetable stock (bouillon) cube
2½ cups/570ml/1 pt boiling spring water
sea salt and freshly ground black pepper

1   Melt the unsalted butter and stir in the flour to form a roux.
2   Take the pan off the heat and stir in the ground almonds, herbs and tamari.
3   Dissolve the stock (bouillon) cube in the boiling water and slowly add to the gravy base, stirring thoroughly and continuously to prevent any lumps forming.
4   Return the pan to the heat and bring gently to the boil, stirring continuously until the mixture thickens. Season to taste.

Freezing:
Can be frozen.

Banana Mêlée Serves 6–8

A variation on a traditional Guernsey dish – usually made with apples, so these have been replaced with bananas instead – really delicious!

½ cup/100g/4 oz unsalted butter
¼ cup/3 tbsps maple syrup
1½ cups/175g/6 oz self-raising wholemeal flour (all-purpose wholewheat flour sifted with 1½ tsps baking powder)

½ tsp freshly grated nutmeg
1 tsp ground (powdered) mixed spice
2¼ lb/1 kg ripe bananas, very thinly sliced

1 Preheat the oven to 190°C/375°F/Gas Mark 5.
2 Melt the unsalted butter in a pan and stir in the maple syrup, then take the pan off the heat and put to one side.
3 Combine the flour and spices in a large bowl and mix in the sliced banana.
4 Add the melted fat and syrup mixture and combine thoroughly to make a sticky consistency.
5 Lightly grease a 22½-cm/9-in flan dish (pie plate), spoon in the mixture and smooth the surface with a knife.
6 Bake for 30–40 minutes until golden brown.

Serve hot or cold with cream or custard. Can also be eaten as a cake – a very useful addition to afternoon tea or the lunch box!

Freezing:
Can be frozen.

Mincemeat Makes about 1.35kg/3 lb

1½ cups/225g/8 oz stoned (pitted) dates
⅔ cup/100g/4 oz dried pears, roughly
   chopped
1 cup/250ml/8 fl oz spring water
1⅓ cups/225g/8 oz sun-dried raisins
1⅓ cups/225g/8 oz sultanas (golden
   seedless raisins)
1⅓ cups/225g/8 oz currants

6 tbsps/75g/3 oz unsalted butter
½ tsp finely grated organic lemon rind
½ tsp finely grated organic orange rind
½ tsp ground (powdered) cinnamon
¼ tsp ground (powdered) nutmeg
⅓–⅔ cup/4–8 tbsps brandy or red grape
   juice, or a mixture of both

1 Place the dates and pears in a pan with the water, cover and bring to
the boil; simmer gently until the pears are tender, the dates very soft
and all the water is absorbed. Leave to cool then chop very finely.
2 Combine thoroughly in a large bowl with all the remaining
ingredients, adding enough brandy or red grape juice to make a moist
but stiff mixture.
3 Cover and leave to stand in a cool place for two days, stirring two or
three times daily, and adding more liquid if required.
4 Press firmly into sterilized glass jars, leaving a 2½ cm/1-in space
at the top.
5 Cover with jam (jelly) pot covers, or screw-on lids, and store in a cool,
dry place.

Mincemeat is best left to mature for 4–5 weeks, then use to make mince
pies, or as a filling in tarts, cakes, etc. It will keep for up to 6 months
without freezing if well sealed, but once opened store in the refrigerator.

Mincemeat and Banana Pie Serves 6–8

This pie is always a favourite – full of flavour

1½ cups/175g/6 oz plain wholemeal (all-purpose wholewheat) flour

1½ cups/175g/6 oz self-raising wholemeal flour (all-purpose wholewheat flour sifted with 1½ tsps baking powder)

pinch sea salt

¾ cup/175g/6 oz unsalted butter

⅔ cup/150ml/¼ pt ice-cold spring water

1lb 2 oz/500g bananas, very thinly sliced

1½ cups/350g/12 oz Mincemeat (see page 215)

Glaze

1 tbsp honey or maple syrup

2 tsps spring water

1   Make the pastry by sifting the flours into a bowl, adding back any separated bran. Mix in a pinch of sea salt, then gently rub the unsalted butter into the flour until the mixture resembles fine breadcrumbs. Add the water and combine to achieve a moist but not too sticky dough (if too moist add extra flour). Cover and chill in the refrigerator for 30 minutes.

2   Preheat the oven to 200°C/400°F/Gas Mark 6.

3   Divide the pastry in two and roll out one half to fit a lightly greased 20-cm/8-in pie dish.

4   Combine the bananas and mincemeat, pile into the prepared pastry base, then roll out the remaining pastry to cover.

5   Make a cross in the centre and decorate with pastry leaves and berries cut from the trimmings.

6   Melt the honey or maple syrup and water together over a low heat and brush as a glaze on top of the pie.

7   Bake for 25–30 minutes, until the pastry is crisp and golden.

Serve with cream or custard (page 220).

Fruity Mincemeat Slice Makes one 900g/2 lb loaf

An extremely moreish fruit slice

1 Preheat the oven to 160°C/325°F/Gas Mark 3.
2 Prepare all the ingredients exactly as for the Mincemeat recipe, page
   215. Place the dates and pears in a saucepan with the water, cover and
   bring to the boil; simmer gently until the pears are tender, the dates
   very soft, and all the water is absorbed. Leave to cool slightly then
   place in a food processor or blender and blend until smooth.
3 Add the unsalted butter and blend again until the ingredients are well
   combined.
4 Combine thoroughly in a large bowl with all the remaining ingredients
   (adding only 4 tbsps/⅓ cup brandy or red grape juice), but with the
   extra addition of 50g/2 oz/½ cup ground almonds, to make a moist
   but stiff mixture.
5 Grease and line the base of a 900g/2 lb loaf tin (pan) with a strip of
   greased lining paper long enough to overhang at both ends.
6 Press the fruit mixture into the tin (pan), then bake uncovered for
   40–50 minutes, or until the top is browned and the loaf feels firm but
   still slightly springy to the touch.

Serve hot or cold as a dessert with custard or cream, or cold as a cake –
it will crumble a little but that does not detract from its delicious flavour!
   The mixture can be made in advance and stored in the refrigerator to
mature for up to 7 days before cooking, if desired.

S
T
A
R
C
H

Bread and Butter Pudding Serves 6

This is a favourite of ours, and we overcame the milk/egg problem so that we can still enjoy it as Hay eaters!

6 tbsps/75g/3 oz unsalted butter, softened
¾ tsp freshly grated nutmeg
¾ tsp ground (powdered) cinnamon
8 slices wholemeal (wholewheat) thick sliced bread, crusts removed
⅓ cup/50g/2 oz currants

⅓ cup/50g/2 oz sultanas (golden seedless raisins)
⅔ cup/150ml/¼ pt double (heavy) cream
6 large egg yolks, beaten
¼ tsp vanilla extract
2 tbsps maple syrup

1 Preheat the oven to 190°C/375°F/Gas Mark 5.
2 Combine the unsalted butter, nutmeg and cinnamon. Spread on each slice of bread then cut into quarters.
3 Arrange a layer of bread over the base of a greased 1½ L/2 pts/5 cups ovenproof dish and sprinkle some of the currants and sultanas (golden seedless raisins) on top.
4 Repeat until all the bread and dried fruit is used up, ending with a layer of bread.
5 Place the cream in a measuring jug and make up to 570ml/1 pt/ 2½ cups with spring water. Transfer to a bowl and whisk in the egg yolks, vanilla extract and maple syrup.
6 Pour the egg and cream mixture over the bread and dried fruit, leave to rest for 10 minutes, then place in the oven and bake uncovered for 35–40 minutes, until golden and crunchy on top.

Fresh Papaya and Sweet Grapes Serves 6

2 lb/900g papaya
1 lb/450g sweet seedless white (green)
    grapes, halved

⅔ cup/100g/4 oz lexia raisins, cooked
    until soft
2 tsps grated organic lemon rind

1   Halve the papaya, scoop out the seeds, peel and then roughly chop the
    flesh and place in a bowl.
2   Add the grapes, raisins and lemon rind and combine.
3   Refrigerate for 1 hour to allow the flavours to blend.

Custard Makes 570ml/1 pt (US 2½ cups)

Another food combining variation avoiding the usual milk component of this all-round favourite food

⅔ cup/150ml/¼ pt double (heavy) cream
2½ cups/570ml/1 pt sachet custard
    powder, or equivalent measure
honey or maple syrup to taste

1 Pour the cream in a measuring jug and make up to 570ml/1 pt/
    2½ cups with spring water.
2 Place the custard powder in a bowl and mix to a paste with a little of
    the diluted cream.
3 Heat the remainder of the diluted cream to nearly boiling point and
    pour on to the custard mix, stirring well.
4 Return the custard to the pan and bring to the boil, stirring
    continuously until the mixture thickens. Sweeten to taste.

Hot Carob Sauce Serves 3–4

A delicious chocolatey alternative!

1¼ cups/175g/6 oz carob drops or pieces
¼ cup/3 tbsps spring water
honey or maple syrup to taste (optional)

1   Pour boiling water into a saucepan and fit a bowl on top, making sure
    it lies above the surface of the water. Place the carob in the bowl and
    leave to melt, stirring occasionally.
2   Add the water and stir until combined.
3   Sweeten, if desired, with honey or maple syrup.

Serve as a sweet fruit or ice-cream topping; lovely with very ripe, sweet
pears and bananas.

Date Sauce Makes 570ml/1 pt (US 2½ cups)

A rich syrupy sauce

1¼ cups/175g/6 oz stoned (pitted) dates
2½ cups/570ml/1 pt spring water

1 Place the dates and water in a pan and bring to the boil.
2 Simmer for 15–20 minutes until tender, then place in a food processor
   or blender and blend until smooth. Add more water, if necessary, for
   the desired consistency.

Serve hot or chilled over sweet fruits or ice-creams.

Variation:
Replace the dates with dried pears or bananas.

The Grant Loaf (with acknowledgements
to Doris Grant) Makes 3 loaves

No food combining cookbook would be complete without giving the recipe for the delicious and easy no-kneading Grant loaf. Since it was first published in *Your Daily Bread* (Faber & Faber, 1944) it has introduced countless families to the pleasure of eating really good wholemeal (wholewheat) bread

12 cups/1.35kg/3 lb stoneground wholemeal (wholewheat) flour
5 cups/1L/2 pts water at blood heat (37°C/98.4°F)

2 tsps sea salt
3 level tsp dried yeast
2 level tsps Barbados sugar, honey or black (blackstrap) molasses

1   Mix the flour with the sea salt (in very cold weather warm flour slightly to take off the chill).
2   Place 3 tbsps of the water in a cup, sprinkle the dried yeast on top and leave for 2 minutes.
3   Add the sugar, honey or molasses. Leave for a further 10–15 minutes by which time there should be a thick creamy froth.
4   Make a well in the centre of the flour and pour in the yeast mixture and the rest of the water.
5   Mix well – by hand is best – for a minute or so, working from sides to middle until the dough feels elastic and leaves the side of the mixing bowl clean. Flours tend to vary in how much water they take up – the dough should be slippery.
6   Divide the dough between three 1½ pts (US 2½ pts) bread tins (pans) which have been warmed and greased.
7   Put the tins (pans) in a warm, not hot, place, cover with a clean cloth and leave for about 20 minutes or until the dough has risen to within 1 cm/½ in of the tops of the tins (pans).
8   Bake in a fairly hot oven, 200°C/400°F/Gas Mark 6, for 35–40 minutes. If the loaf sounds hollow when the top is knocked, it is done.

Freezing:
It makes good sense to bake three loaves because the bread freezes excellently.

Suggestions for Packed Meals

This is the simplest packed Hay meal to prepare, using the very familiar sandwich. There is, however, plenty of scope for other starch dishes and these, as well as some sandwich filling ideas, are given below:

- New potatoes
- Dips and pâtés with bread, crackers, crispbreads, oatcakes, etc.
- Slices of cold vegetable flan or nutloaf
- Rice or pasta salad
- Soup
- Vegetable pasty
- Muesli (granola) served with diluted cream

Sandwich Fillers

- Salad
- Coleslaw
- Banana and cinnamon
- Sweetcorn and spring onion (scallion)
- Grated courgette (shredded zucchini) with chopped tomato and marjoram
- Finely chopped celery and grated (shredded) carrot
- Mashed cooked dates flavoured with grated organic orange rind
- Cream cheese and garlic or mixed herbs
- Cucumber and chopped walnuts with finely grated organic lemon rind
- Olives and cucumber
- Hard-boiled egg yolk and chopped fresh parsley

To follow, pack any of the sweet fruits such as bananas, figs, dates, etc. or make up a small container of currants, sun-dried raisins and sultanas (golden seedless raisins). Compatible wholemeal (wholewheat) cakes or biscuits are also suitable for this meal.

Seasonal Menu Planner

SPRING MENUS FOR ONE WEEK

	BREAKFAST	MIDDAY	EVENING
Sunday	**A** Fresh grapefruit sections	**P** Easy Tarragon Chicken (p 109) French Beans Spring Carrots Mixed Green Salad Spiced Apple Fool (p 148)	**S** Mushroom and Tarragon Bake (p 199) New Potato, Spring Onion/Scallion and Red Pepper Salad (p 182) Fresh Papaya

Note: on a Sunday, the breakfast and midday menu could be combined as "brunch"

	BREAKFAST	MIDDAY	EVENING
Monday	**A** Orange Sections with Yoghurt	**S** Tarragon, Leek and Potato Soup (p 173) Wholemeal/wheat roll Very sweet ripe pear	**P** Cream of Chicken (p 110) Stir-Fried Courgettes (p 135) Chicory and Orange Salad (p 86) Fresh Fruit of choice
Tuesday	**A** Junket (p 56) with fruit of choice	**P** Mixed Green Salad Cubes of Cheddar Cheese Dessert Apples	**S** Curried Jacket Potato (p 205) Steamed carrots and broccoli Mincemeat and Banana Pie with cream (p 216)
Wednesday	**S** Roasted Buckwheat and Pear Porridge (p 167)	**A** Parsnip and Apple Soup (p 36) Courgette/Zucchini and Carrot Salad (p 39) Orange Sections	**P** Lemon Sole with Dill (p 104) Celeriac Purée (p 132) Fennel and Radish Salad Spiced Apricot Mousse (p 153)
Thursday	**A** Lightly Stewed Apples with Raisins and Yoghurt	**P** Creamy Celery and Walnut Soup (p 75) Egg and Tomato Salad (p 98) Winter Fruit Compote (p 157)	**S** Vegetable and Borlotti/Pinto Bean Lasagne (p 196) Garlic Bread Salad Very sweet ripe grapes
Friday	**A** Soaked Dried Apricots with Wheatgerm and Yoghurt	**S** Banana and Fig Muesli Wholemeal/wheat roll and butter Very sweet ripe pear	**P** Trout Fillets poached in Cider (p 101) Creamed Swiss Chard (p 131) Baked apple with cream
Saturday	**A** Fresh melon	**P** Avocado and Grapefruit Salad (p 95) Mushroom Omelette Mousseline (p 120) Mixed Green Salad Fresh Fruit of choice	**S** Cauliflower Cheese (p 188) Sesame Potatoes (p 209) Green salad Grilled Mushrooms Stewed dried pears, dates, figs and raisins with Custard (p 219)

	BREAKFAST	MIDDAY	EVENING
Sunday	**A** Fresh Raspberries with Natural Yoghurt	**P** Coriander Lamb (p 113) Steamed Peas and Finger Carrots with butter Green Salad Strawberries and Cream	**S** Cold Cheesy Carrot and Potato Pie (p 192) Green Salad Sweet fresh fruit of choice

Note: on a Sunday, the breakfast and midday menus could be combined as "brunch"

Monday	**A** Ripe Peach with Yoghurt	**A** Apple, Raisin and Cream Cheese Salad on a bed of lettuce Sliced Nectarine with Crème Fraîche	**P** Chilled Courgette/ Zucchini Soup (p 71) Chicken Breasts (p 111) Steamed Buttered Peas Green Salad Bowl of Cherries
Tuesday	**A** Dr Bircher's Muesli (p 31)	**P** Egg and Tomato Salad (p 98) Fresh Fruit in Season, e.g. raspberries, peaches or nectarines	**S** Lentil and Herb Burgers (p 201) New potatoes and salad Very ripe sweet pear
Wednesday	**A** Fresh grapefruit and orange segments	**S** Wholemeal/wheat banana sandwiches Raw tomato and sticks of cucumber Very sweet ripe grapes	**A** Salad à la Guacamole (p 40) Junket with sliced peaches (p 56)
Thursday	**S** Chopped banana with 1 tbsp wheatgerm Milk or yoghurt	**P** Chicken Salad with Herb Dressing (p 96) Carrot, Apple and Raisin Salad (p 85) Fresh Fruit	**A** Savoury Lettuce Soup (p 37) Steamed Baby Cauliflower with a little melted butter Chopped Apple and Diced Pineapple served with cream
Friday	**A** A dessert pear sliced and sprinkled with 1 dsp sunflower seeds topped with yoghurt	**S** Wholemeal/wheat crispbread Minty Pea and Lemon Pasta Salad (p 184) Nuts and Raisins	**P** Marinated Courgette/ Zucchini (p 79) Sea Bass with Tarragon (p 105) Steamed Peas and Creamy Carrot Purée Sliced Nectarines laced with Raspberries (p 149)
Saturday	**A** Fresh Fruit Salad	**P** Chilled Cucumber Soup (p 72) Courgette/Zucchini Omelette (p 119) Green Salad Summer Fruit Compote (p 147)	**S** Braised Savoury Mushrooms (p 175) Jacket Potato Tomato and Onion Salad Banana and cold Custard (p 219)

	BREAKFAST	MIDDAY	EVENING
Sunday	**A** Citrus Fruit and Apple (p 27)	**P** Green Salad Casserole of Pheasant in Red Wine (p 112) Steamed French Beans Crispy Oven Parsnips Spiced Apple Fool (p 148)	**S** Onion and Sweetcorn Soup (p 171) Wholemeal/wheat bread Fruity Mincemeat Slice (p 217)

Note: on a Sunday, the breakfast and midday menu could be combined as "brunch"

	BREAKFAST	MIDDAY	EVENING
Monday	**A** Fresh fruit in season with yoghurt	**S** Pumpkin Soup (p 174) Salad Sandwiches Fresh Figs with a little crème fraîche	**P** Tarragon Baked Eggs (p 117) Grilled Nutbrown Mushrooms (p 134) Carrot, Apple and Raisin Salad (p 85) Sliced Oranges
Tuesday	**A** Melon Crush (p 28)	**P** Halibut Salad with crisp lettuce (p 102) Ripe dessert pear	**A** Cream of Leek Soup (p 33) Buttered Chicory Steamed Mangetout Peas Fresh Fruit
Wednesday	**S** Oatmeal Porridge (p 165)	**A** Apple and Avocado Salad (p 38) Fresh Pineapple Slices with Crème Fraîche	**P** Courgette/Zucchini and Carrot Soup (p 73) Chicken Salad with Herb Dressing (p 96) Dessert Apples and Raisins
Thursday	**A** Stewed Apple sprinkled with cinnamon and ginger	**P** Tomato Cups (p 77) Cauliflower and Parsnip Soup (p 74) Apples	**S** Onion and Oregano Flan (p 189) New potatoes Buttered carrots Very sweet ripe grapes
Friday	**A** Orange juice Pineapple, Apricot and Sultana Muesli (p 29)	**S** Wholemeal/wheat roll and butter Rice Salad with Orange, Date and Sweetcorn (p 183) Dried pears	**P** Poached Brill with a Green Sauce (p 107) Creamed Swiss Chard (p 131) Mixed Green Salad Spiced Apricot Mousse (p 153)
Saturday	**S** Banana and Fig Muesli (p 168)	**A** Fresh Pineapple Salad (p 41) Nuts and Raisins	**P** Chicory and Orange Salad Venison with Soured Cream (p 115) Buttered, steamed cauliflower or broccoli Celeriac Purée (p 132) Autumn Fruit Compote (p 150)

	BREAKFAST	MIDDAY	EVENING
Sunday	**A** Fresh ruby grapefruit and orange sections	**P** Lamb cutlets (p 114) or Scrambled Eggs (p 118) with mushrooms and tomatoes Spiced Red Cabbage and Walnut Salad (p 88) Baked Apple and Almond Pudding (p 152)	**S** Hearty Vegetable Soup (p 172) Wholemeal/wheat roll and butter Banana and fresh papaya

Note: on a Sunday, the breakfast and midday menu could be combined as "brunch"

Monday	**A** Greek yoghurt with 1 tsp honey and 1 tbsp chopped almonds and sesame seeds	**S** Salad sandwiches made with wholemeal bread Few fresh dates	**P** Aubergines stuffed with Cheese (p 123) Basic Green Salad (p 10) Bunch of grapes
Tuesday	**S** Oatmeal Porridge (p 165) served with top milk	**A** Parsnip and Apple Soup (p 36) Winter Beet Salad (p 43) An orange	**P** Creamed Smoked Haddock (p 103) Steamed Peas and Calabrese Florets Spiced Pears (p 151)
Wednesday	**A** Hunza apricots soaked overnight, served hot and topped with yoghurt	**S** Wholemeal/wholewheat sandwiches with cream cheese and herbs Sticks of celery Mixture of raisins and sultanas/golden seedless raisins	**P** Avocados with Walnuts (p 97) Cold sliced ham with Chicory and Orange Salad (p 86) Baked Apples stuffed with raisins and honey
Thursday	**S** 2 tbsps oatflakes soaked overnight in spring water, add chopped banana and a little top milk or yoghurt	**A** End of Winter Soup (p 34) Winter Crunch Salad (p 42) Apples	**S** Baked Jacket Potato with butter Grilled mushrooms Mixed Green Salad Bread and Butter Pudding (p 218)
Friday	**A** A dessert pear sliced and sprinkled with 1 dsp sunflower seeds topped with yoghurt	**S** Leek and Carrot Pastie (p 186) Mixed salad Dried figs and dates	**P** Mixed Vegetable Frittata (p 121) Green Salad (p 10) Spiced Apple Fool (p 148)
Saturday	**A** Bircher Muesli (p 31)	**P** Grilled Salmon Steaks with Dill (p 108) Creamed Swiss Chard (p 131) Winter Fruit Compote (p 157)	**S** Wholemeal/wheat crackers and Humous (p 178) Green salad Slice of Banana Mêlée (p 214)

Food Combining for Health Cookbook

Bibliography and Further Reading

Food Combining: The Hay System

Doris Grant and Jean Joice, *Food Combining for Health* (Thorsons, 1984)

Jackie Habgood, *The Hay Diet Made Easy* (Souvenir Press, 1997)

—, *Get Well with the Hay Diet* (Souvenir Press, 1999)

William Howard Hay, *A New Health Era* (Harrap; out of print but secondhand copies are sometimes available)

Jackie Le Tissier, *Food Combining for Vegetarians* (Thorsons, 1992)

Erwina Lidolt, *The Food Combining Cookbook* (Thorsons, 1987)

Other Food Combining Systems

Harvey and Marilyn Diamond, *Fit for Life* (Bantam, 1987)

Marilyn Diamond, *The Fit for Life Cookbook* (Bantam, 1990)

—, *A New Way of Eating* (Bantam, 1987)

Leslie Kenton, *The Biogenic Diet* (Century, 1984)

Kathryn Marsden, *The Food Combining Diet* (Thorsons, 1993)

—, *Food Combining in 30 Days* (Thorsons, 1994)

—, *The Food Combiner's Meal Planner* (Thorsons, 1994)

Tim Spong and Vicki Peterson, *Food Combining* (Prism Press, 1993)

Michael Van Straten and Barbara Griggs, *Super Foods* (Dorling Kindersley, 1990)

—, *The Super Foods Diet Book* (Dorling Kindersley, 1992)

Celia Wright, *The Wright Diet* (Piatkus, 1986)

Eating for Health: Wholefood Cookbooks

Lynda Brown, *Fresh Thoughts on Food* (Dorling Kindersley, 1988)

Sophie Grigson, *Eat Your Greens* (Network Books, 1993)

Jane Grigson, *Jane Grigson's Vegetable Book* (Penguin, 1980)

—, *Jane Grigson's Fruit Book* (Penguin, 1988)

Susan Hicks, *The Fish Course* (BBC, 1987)

Elbie Lebrecht, *Sugar-Free Desserts, Drinks and Ices* (Faber & Faber, 1993)

—, *Sugar-Free Cooking* (Thorsons, 1994)
Nigel Slater, *Real Fast Food* (Penguin, 1993)
Sarah Woodward, *Fresh from the Market* (Macmillan, 1993)

Vegetarian Cookbooks
Any books by Rose Elliot, but in particular
Rose Elliot, *Rose Elliot's Vegetarian Four Seasons* (HarperCollins, 1993).
    Includes a Food Combining Index.
—, *Rose Elliot's Complete Vegetarian Cookbook* (Collins, 1985)
Deborah Madison with Edward Espe Brown, *The Greens Cook Book* (Bantam,
    1987)
Stephanie Segal, *The Winter Vegetarian* (Papermac, 1989)
—, *The Summer Vegetarian* (Papermac, 1991)
(These last two titles contain good recipes, especially for soup, easily
    adaptable for the Hay System)

Raw Foods, Herbs and Salads, Grow your Own
Lynda Brown, *The Cook's Garden* (Century, 1990)
Leslie and Susannah Kenton, *Raw Energy* (Century, 1984)
Joy Larkom, *The Salad Garden* (Windward, 1984)
—, *Oriental Vegetables* (John Murray, 1991)

General Health Interest
T. L. Cleave, *The Saccharine Disease* (John Wright & Sons, 1974)
Barbara Griggs, *The Food Factor* (Penguin, 1989)
Walter Yellowlees, *A Doctor in the Wilderness* (Janus Publishing, 1993)
John Yudkin, *Pure White and Deadly: The Problem of Sugar* (Penguin, 1988)

Combined Index

Alkaline Index

Protein Index

Starch Index

aubergine (eggplant), mushroom
    and lentil curry 187

bananas
  banana and fig muesli (granola)
    168
  banana mêlée 214
  banana and papaya cream 166
  mincemeat and banana pie 216
bean jar 200
braised savoury mushrooms 175
bread and butter pudding 218
breakfasts 165–70
broccoli and courgette (zucchini)
    rice baked in leek and nutmeg
    sauce 190
buckwheat, roasted buckwheat and
    pear porridge 167

carrots, cheesy carrot and potato
    pie 192
cauliflower cheese 188
cereals 163
cheese
  cheesy carrot and potato pie 192
  macaroni cheese 203
chestnut, mushroom and orange
    stir 179
corn on the cob
  baby corn with peppers in onion
    and garlic dressing 181
  corn with mixed spice and
    nutmeg butter 176

courgettes (zucchini)
  courgette (zucchini) and
    aubergine (eggplant) flan 193
  courgette (zucchini) and red
    pepper pizza 202
cream 163
cream cheese sauce 210
curried jacket potatoes 205
custard 219

dairy products 163
date sauce 222
desserts 214–23
Doris Grant loaf 223
drinks 164

first courses 175–81
fresh papaya and sweet grapes
    219
fruits 164
  fruity mincemeat slice 217

grains 163
gravies 213

haricot beans, herby haricot (navy)
    beans 177
hearty vegetable soup 172
herbs 163
  herby haricot (navy) beans 177
hot carob sauce 221
humous 178
  humous green beans 208